To Nanna and Poppa

CONTENTS

1

THE SMOKE

A bead of sweat dropped from Charlie's brow. It splattered in the middle of the exam paper, expanding the puddle created by previous drops.

Charlie's throat muscles tightened. His heartbeat thumped. He knew this math exam was important. Tugging hard at his fringe, he read Question Eight again — *finish the line graph by plotting the point 22, 16.*

Jeepers, thought Charlie. *How do I do that?*

With his brain cells swirling, the gridlines on the paper blurred. His eyes started straining and his thoughts went fuzzy. *Who does this weird kind of stuff anyway? … and why?*

He spotted the wall clock, right above Mrs. Grimshaw's head. Eleven o'clock and only one hour to go. A burning feeling began on the left side of his chest.

'Great,' said Charlie under his breath. 'Now I'm having a heart attack.'

His mind started to play tricks on him. The sensation in his chest just got hotter. In the midst of a scorching ribcage stab, he spied a narrow plume of smoke coming from the top pocket of his school blazer.

Yikes! Charlie's fingers wrangled his pocket open. *I'm on fire!*

Through a thin haze, Charlie eyeballed the source. Ted's key. The *Eternal Key*. Smoking like a chimney from his uniform.

Charlie had only put the Key in his pocket earlier that morning — thinking it would bring him luck. He needed all the help he could get.

Trying to seal the smoke in with one hand, he pressed the pocket firmly against his chest. The other hand darted skyward, as he made eye contact with Mrs. Grimshaw.

'Err… Excuse me… Ma'am.'

The class turned their heads and glared at Charlie.

'Yes, Charlie,' said Mrs. Grimshaw.

'Can I be excused to the bathroom?'

'*Really,* Charlie.' Mrs. Grimshaw's eyes narrowed into slits. 'You should have thought of that before.'

'Please, Ma'am — it's urgent.'

Muffled giggles rang out across the school hall.

'Alright then.' The teacher rolled her eyes.

Charlie jumped from his seat, and made a bee-line for the bathroom at the rear of the building. Dashing into a tiny restroom, he slammed the door behind him and clipped the inside lock.

Grabbing the Key from his pocket, Charlie tossed it into the basin.

Clang.

The Key spun around the ceramic as if it was under a spell. More smoke poured from the Key as it pulsed up and down.

Quickly, Charlie flicked on the tap. Water gushed from the spout, but the liquid never touched the Key. It was like there was some kind of invisible shield around the shiny gold. Charlie glared at the Key as the water vanished down the drain hole.

Charlie studied the Key's movements. It glowed orange and bulged out, changed colour to yellow and shrunk. Then glowed orange again, bulged out, back to yellow and shrunk. An odd stench filled the air. Not a wood scented smoke like you would expect, more of a chemical smell, like a suffocating gas. Charlie's breathing became heavier.

From the intricate carvings etched into the shiny gold, Charlie watched the smoke overflow from the basin. It started to fill the bathroom. A wave of confusion set into Charlie's head. *What is going on?*

'Everything alright in there?' Hollered Mrs. Grimshaw from the other side of the door.

'Yep — all good!' shouted Charlie. He bit his lip.

Suddenly, the smoke thickened. It billowed with force away from the Key and started to pressurise the bathroom walls, putting huge cracks in them.

Whoa, thought Charlie. *I need to get this Key outside.*

Spying a window above the toilet, Charlie jumped up onto the toilet lid. He shoved the glass pane open and whacked a fly screen off with his fist. Leaping back to the basin, he wrapped his fingers around the Key.

In that split second, a sharp pain stabbed him under the skin of his hand. His fingers throbbed in agony. A strange image appeared on the Key, that wasn't there before. A picture of a sun became visible, and underneath it, a simple cross. The lines of the cross flashed a luminous green. Charlie tried to toss the Key through the window, but it was stuck — super-glued to his hand.

Panicked, Charlie stumbled backwards onto the basin and hit his head. He landed hard on the tiled floor. The smoke whooshed from the Key and raged with anger.

Charlie watched the cracks in the walls get bigger. Next minute, one entire wall of the bathroom blew out. Then another fell. Then another. Crouching under the basin, Charlie covered his head as the roof blew off. The whole bathroom box collapsed like a house of cards. But where was the oval next to the school? Not there. Nothing there. Just space. Black space.

Pulling him like a rag doll, the Key began to lift Charlie's body, the tiles dissolved under his feet. He gripped the Key tightly, as if hanging onto life. With the Key dragging him higher, he speared into space.

2

THE ETERNAL WORLD

As the Key twisted Charlie higher, space somehow became darker. Charlie saw a tiny white ball of light appear in the distance. The ball grew larger, like an expanding sphere of electricity. It looked as though it was heading straight for him — on a collision course.

The electrically charged ball rocketed towards Charlie. And Charlie rocketed towards it. Screaming his lungs out, Charlie shut his eyes and held his breath. But then, his body suddenly jolted to a stop. Charlie felt his legs floating.

At that moment, Charlie knew he had entered a new realm — a world that seemed familiar. He knew where he was, because he had been there before. It was a special place. A sudden peacefulness came over him. A feeling of the *Eternal World*.

Memories of Ted flooded back to Charlie. He remembered the day his grandfather died, when he saw his mum and dad crying on the couch. He recalled the funeral with all Ted's friends, most of them Charlie didn't know, and the big black car that took them to the cemetery.

In the weeks that followed Ted's passing, Charlie had waited for a sign from his grandfather. A sign to let him know that Ted was alright. But there was no sign. Nothing came from the stars or the heavens. But then, that all changed. Charlie visited Ted in the Eternal World. Ted was happy, his face youthful and fresh. He remembered when he first saw the Eternal Key, radiating pure light like a star.

Slowly, Charlie opened his eyes. The giant sphere crackled right in front of his nose. Particles inside the sphere looked like electrons spinning around a nucleus. Electromagnetic waves shot out at Charlie's head. He couldn't move. Stuck in some kind of weird magnetic field.

Whack.

A thunderbolt crackled from the ball and ignited the Key. An electric shock ran up a vein in Charlie's arm, causing his shoulder to shudder. In silence, he watched the gigantic atom's protons and neutrons buzzing rhythmically. Then suddenly, the infrared rays reversed direction and collapsed into the nucleus. From the energy mass, a body emerged and grinned.

'Hello, Charlie.'

'Ted!' Charlie's eyes sparkled. 'It's been months.'

Ted stepped forward and threw his arms around his dearest grandson.

Tears welled in Charlie's eyes. A lump caught in his throat.

'Nice to see you again.' With a lift of his hand, Ted gently touched Charlie on the cheek. 'I have been looking for you.'

Charlie gazed at his grandfather for a minute, wishing that Ted was back in his life permanently. But then he noticed huge dark rings, like truck tyres, circling Ted's eyes. Even his rosy skin had turned a pasty grey that looked as though it could flake off at any time. Deep cavernous lines stretched across his forehead.

'Are you alright, Ted?' asked Charlie.

'You are looking good, Charlie,' Ted wheezed.

'Ted, what's wrong?'

Pausing for a second, Ted gave Charlie an anxious look. He started to speak, but instead exhaled a raspy cough. 'I am alright.' He coughed again. 'Really.'

Charlie didn't buy it.

Ted cleared his throat and spoke slowly and with purpose. 'Charlie, you are here in the Eternal World because I need your help.'

'Help?'

'I need you to do something for me.'

'What is it, Ted?'

'The *Key*, Charlie, the *Eternal Key*.'

'Yes, Ted, I have the Key here.' Charlie unravelled the Key from his fingers. 'It started smoking in the exam… I thought it was going to burn down the school hall.'

'Ahhh…' Ted smiled at the Key as Charlie passed it to him.

Tiny wafts of smoke still coming from the gold drifted towards Ted's colourless face. Charlie noticed that the strange images were still on the Key — the picture of the sun and the cross flashing a luminous green.

'Beautiful, isn't it?' whispered Ted.

Charlie nodded.

'Just beautiful,' said Ted again. He raised the Key to eye level and the ions and electrons began zapping again in Ted's hand, as though he was re-charging it. Ted examined the gold leaf, the sun engraving, and the cross flickering green.

Charlie watched his grandfather scrutinise the Key. It reminded him of the days they spent together in the museum. Those warm Sunday afternoons in the basement. Ted wearing his white gloves as he sipped tea, studying the latest artefact. Ted had such a keen eye for detail, he could see things that no one else could see. Little markings, little scratches, little stamps that on the face of it meant nothing but could really tell you everything.

Charlie remembered Ted pulling out special objects from under his desk — a locked box, a locked trunk, a locked something from deep within the archives. Every weekend the challenge was different. With his wire in hand, Charlie would get to work. Sometimes it would take him hours and hours to pick the locks. But he always got them open. Distant memories though now, and even today, Ted seemed as distant as the memories.

'Ted, you said that you needed my help?' said Charlie.

Out of his trance, Ted nodded. He passed the Key back to his grandson. 'Charlie, when you came here last time, to the Eternal World, and I gave you this Key… You became something special.'

'I did?'

'Yes, you became the *Keyholder*.'

'The Keyholder.' Charlie twirled the Key between his fingers.

'Yes. It is a powerful and important position, and one that comes with responsibility.'

Charlie studied the Key. He wasn't a big fan of powerful and important positions, especially if they came with responsibility.

'As the Keyholder, you now have an obligation to

a higher calling.'

'A calling… What calling?' Charlie scratched his head and thought, *this does not sound good.*

Ted paused for a second. 'The truth.'

Dark looming space gases suddenly went darker. Ted eyed the black vapours as though he was challenging them for a fight. His voice firmed. 'A calling to find *the truth.*'

'What are you talking about Ted? I don't understand.'

'Charlie, the Key in your hand seeks out the most powerful thing of all. It looks for the very thing we all want in our lives,' Ted rasped. '…And in death. It searches for the one thing that rises above everything else. It searches for the truth.'

Charlie started to think that Ted had lost the plot.

'The truth about what?' he asked.

'About everything. The truth about everything.'

Charlie stared at the Key.

'Charlie you are the Keyholder for a reason. There is something special about you — you have a certain quality that is very important.'

'I do?'

'Yes, Charlie, goodness.' Ted smiled at Charlie with pride. 'When you went to Ancient Greece and met with Plato and the Oracle, they saw it too. They saw goodness in you and goodness in your soul. You have an ability to put wrong things right. The Key was smoking today, because it senses wrong-doing. And as the Keyholder, you have an obligation. You have to find the wrong-doing, and correct it.'

Dark murky gasses moved in, circling Charlie and Ted like a predator. Charlie sensed a fierce storm was about to whip up, and he and Ted were in the epicentre.

'There is a man called Descartes, and like Plato, he is a philosopher. Descartes is in trouble. He wrote a manuscript called *Meditations*.'

'A manuscript?'

'A book Charlie, and this is no ordinary book. It is a book about the foundations of human knowledge. It is a book about a process we can follow to know the truth about our world. I cannot stress enough how important this manuscript is. But there is a problem — it has been stolen.'

'Stolen? By who?'

'By evil, Charlie — by an evil demon.'

'You're kidding, right?'

Charlie grinned, hoping that Ted was kidding, but something about the supernatural clouds swirling violently around his head made him think that he wasn't.

'No, I am not kidding Charlie. I wish I was. This demon is powerful and cunning. It is not of your world.' Ted looked uneasy. 'The demon has lived in Descartes' thoughts for some time. But recently, it's getting more powerful. It's feeding off Descartes' ideas in his book. The ideas give the demon energy, make it stronger. Now it's trying to control Descartes' mind.'

'How do you know that?' asked Charlie.

'The demon came here, to see me.'

'You.' Charlie gulped. 'The demon came to see you in the Eternal World?'

'Yes,' said Ted. 'The mind and the soul are connected. They are made of the same substance. With enough energy, the demon can move between them both. It can visit the soul.'

'But why did it come to see you, Ted?'

'Why me?' Ted paused. 'I really don't know.'

'What did it do?'

'It flashed Descartes' book in front of my face, told me it was going to control everyone, and shrieked out a bloodcurdling laugh. Then it zapped me, sucking energy from me, making me sick. I thought it would go away. But it didn't. It just kept coming back, zapping me again and again. Now it is attacking my friends here, sucking energy from them, making them sick as well.'

'How do you stop it?'

'I can't stop it. I spend my days hiding from it in this atom. But it always finds me.'

'*You* have to stop it Charlie,' wheezed Ted.

'Me,' gasped Charlie. 'Stopping a demon?'

'You.'

'But how?'

'Go to the source its feeding on. Find Descartes and his stolen book.'

Charlie shook his head in disbelief.

Ted's eyes focused on the Key. 'As the Keyholder, the Key can take you to places you didn't think possible. But be careful. The demon will try and stop you at every turn. Follow your instincts, follow your thoughts. The demon cannot win this. You have to find that book, and get it back to Descartes.'

'But Ted, what if I can't find Descartes, or the book?'

'You have to, Charlie.' Ted fell silent.

'But what if I can't?'

'Charlie, if you don't, the demon will control us all.' Ted's pupils dilated and he scanned the skies, as though he was looking for something in particular.

'Hurry, the process has started,' urged Ted. 'And remember, the Key can take you anywhere.'

'But Ted, what about you?' Tears began to form again in Charlie's eyes. 'You're sick… Really sick.'

'Find the book, Charlie, return it to Descartes and I will get better,' said Ted. 'We will all get better.'

In that instant, a power surge blasted from the Key. An electrical current ripped up Charlie's arm across his rib cage into his organs. The force threw him backwards into the swirling vapours. He stumbled, holding onto his chest. Then, speckled throughout space, Charlie saw a thousand faces strangely illuminated like tiny stars. But all peering down at him, with grey sickly faces and black truck-tyre eyes — just like Ted's.

'My friends.' Ted pondered the ghostly faces in the sky and took in a deep breath. 'Let the Key guide you Charlie. Follow the path of truth.'

A painful knot twisted inside Charlie's gut. It felt like the electric current had somehow managed to strike the lining of his stomach. Now the damage was spreading from his gut, through his lower rib cage, up towards his heart.

'Goodbye, Charlie.' Ted placed a heavy hand on Charlie's shoulder. 'And good luck.'

In what looked like excruciating pain, Ted shuffled forward, wincing over every step, and hugged his grandson. His smile appeared strained and unconvincing.

That smile is not filled with happiness, thought Charlie, *it's full of fear*. And now that fear was inside Charlie, burning him up like a wildfire in his core.

Overhead, the dark ominous clouds started to bubble over and swallow the faces. Turning his back on Charlie, Ted began to stagger away. Limping and sluggish, it was agonising for Charlie to watch. Ted looked as though he had forgotten how to operate his own limbs.

Charlie hated to see his grandfather like this. It reminded him of when Ted was in hospital, just before he died. Not able to move, not able to speak. Ted had become a frail old man, unrecognisable to the man he once was.

'Wait, Ted!' screamed Charlie, tears streaming. 'Wait!'

Violent winds swirled around his grandfather and the magnetic field ignited. Protons and electrons shot sparks at Charlie's head again, just as the giant charged atom swallowed Ted.

'No!' cried Charlie. 'Come back!'

Fierce winds blustered Charlie's hair as his blazer flapped. In seconds, the ball zoomed away from him, until he could only see a tiny spec of light glowing on the edge of space.

Crack.

A lightning bolt shot out of the distant ball and hit the Key in Charlie's tight-fisted grip. His body flipped backwards.

In pitch blackness and with no oxygen, Charlie dropped like a rock. He plummeted through the rumbling air. He couldn't think. He couldn't breathe. His heartbeat stopped. Into a free form nose-dive, Charlie plunged. He smashed onto rock-hard ground.

3

THE TRAPDOOR

Lying on his stomach, Charlie lifted his head and spat dirt from his mouth. A sharp razor-like pain darted down his neck. He turned his head sideways. Battering his eyelids open, he spotted a faint orange glow. He guessed it was the Key. Lunging at his lifeline, he snatched it up into his icy cold palm. Heat oozed from the Key and warmed Charlie's hand as he watched the glow of the orange metal turn into a torch-like yellow. He raised the Key above his head, casting light on the dirt surrounding him. Trapped in a hole underground, he flashed the Key in front of him. He saw a narrow tunnel.

Sucking in a load of freezing cold air, Charlie squeezed through the burrow, nearly crushing his shoulder blades. Gritting his teeth, he scraped skin from his elbows as he went. Sweat dripped from his forehead as dust wrestled his eyes. He squirmed forward. His breath became heavier. Just as the grime in his eyes was about to glue his lashes, a trapdoor appeared at the end of the tunnel ahead. Charlie wriggled with purpose towards it.

With a tight fist, Charlie rammed the timber flap open. He slipped through a hole and dropped to the floor. Dazed and disorientated, Charlie clambered to his feet and stood in an icebox of a room, barely lit by a dirty window high above his head. He arched out his lower back and stretched. The Key in his hand shed some light around him — and that's when he noticed his shoes.

'You're kidding,' he whispered to himself.

Long black leathers with a point at the end you could kill someone with. They had ribbons too, a silky mauve colour, like the type a girl would put in her hair — not a ribbon that belonged to the shoes of a boy. But not only was he wearing weird ugly shoes, he was wearing weird ugly socks too. Horrible ones. White with fine darn and pulled to his knee, in a stretchy material like stockings, only thicker.

Panicked, he flashed the Key on his body. Instead of seeing his blazer, he saw a purple velvet jacket with a row of gold stitched buttons on the front. Grey balloon pants made him look like he was double his size, and stopped just above his knees. He rubbed the velvety material with his palms. *Blimey, I look like a clown*. He gulped.

When he had forgotten about his horrible fashion sense, Charlie shone the Key upwards, towards the roof. Coarse little bricks lined a high arched ceiling. He shivered. A weird odour drifted up his nostrils. He recognised the smell. He experienced it every time he went into Mr. Romano's butcher shop... meat... raw meat. The kind of smell that hangs in the air, gets into your clothes, and stays there long after you leave the shop. He moved faster between the thick timber shelves, flashing the Key as he went.

'Arrrgh!' He screamed and jumped backwards.

A giant trout dangled from a hook.

His heart thumped.

'This is not good,' he whispered.

Backing away, Charlie spied a raw leg of lamb on a shelf. Next to it, a tray of uncooked chicken legs and a box of cabbages. Then he noticed a small barrel at the end of the shelves piled high with kidneys and gizzards. He guessed he was in a food cellar.

Whoosh.

A noise came from behind him. He saw a flicker of light. Quickly, he slipped the Key down the front of his purple jacket. Petrified and hearing only the sound of his own heavy breathing, he crept behind the dark shadows of the shelves.

Whoosh.

The noise again! Straining his ears and eyes, he ducked behind the barrel with the gizzards, too frightened to breathe.

Whack.

Something sharp struck his throat. A force grabbed his right arm and twisted it high up his back.

'Move, and I will kill you,' hissed a girl's voice in his ear, in an unfamiliar accent.

The blade of the knife spiked into his neck. He couldn't turn his head.

'You are on my patch — I do not like it when strangers are on my patch.'

Charlie felt the girl's hot breath against his earlobe.

'I… I can't breathe,' he spluttered. He tried to release his arm.

'Why are you here?' snarled the voice.

Charlie gasped for air. 'Let me go. You're hurting me!'

She twisted his limb higher and moved her face into his. 'Answer the question!'

Charlie could see the girl's blackened face out of the corner of his eye. She screwed up her stubby nose as her sparkling green irises rolled over Charlie's body like Mrs. Grimshaw does when his shirt is not tucked in. All of a sudden, he became very self-conscious standing in front of this strange dirty girl in his dumb velvet costume with even dumber pointed shoes.

'Err… I'm looking for someone,' blurted Charlie.

'Down here?' The girl frowned. 'In the cellar?'

Charlie felt the blade pressing harder against his throat.

'Stealing food, more like.'

'No, really,' cried Charlie. 'I wasn't stealing food — I'm looking for someone.'

'*Who?*' snorted the girl.

'A man called Descartes.'

'Descartes?' The girl's voice became softer. 'The Queen's philosopher… What do you want with the Frenchman?'

French, thought Charlie. *Ted didn't mention he was French. And he didn't mention anything about a Queen.*

'I just need to find him,' he said. 'Do you know him?'

'I know everyone,' said the girl confidently, like she actually did know everyone in the world.

'Will you take me to him?' Charlie studied the girl's enlarged pupils and hoped that she would take him to Descartes — or at least get the knife off his neck.

The girl shot an odd glance back at Charlie and smiled. Her teeth gleamed like white pearls against the brown grime concealing her skin. She flicked her long hair dropping from a ragged woollen beanie.

'Depends on what you are paying.' She pressed

the blade harder.

Money, he thought. *She wants money.*

Frantically, he moved his hand from the blade, and fingered his way around his balloon pants hoping to find a coin or two in his pocket, or anything of value — but nothing. He gazed at the girl with his hound dog eyes, the same look he gave his mum when he was in trouble, and said, 'I can't pay you. I have no money.'

'I will take your watch,' she said in a flash.

Charlie knew he didn't have his watch on. 'I haven't got a watch,' he said.

'Do not lie to me,' barked the girl.

Pulling the knife away from Charlie's neck, the girl stepped forward. With the tip of the blade she tapped a chain, that only now Charlie noticed was clipped to a button on his jacket. She pulled down on the chain.

A round brass container fell from his upper top pocket and dangled on the other end of the chain. With her grubby little fingers, she flipped open the lid and Charlie saw a strange clock face, with only one hand — not two. The brass flashed under the light of the window.

Nothing about the watch — if that's what it was — looked normal to Charlie. He was just about to rip it from his jacket and give it to the girl, but an alarm bell went off in his head. *What if she just takes off with it?*

What if she doesn't even take me to Descartes? She hardly seems trustworthy.

'I'll give you my watch when I meet Descartes,' he said.

Charlie felt much better about this plan. The girl twitched up her nose and narrowed her eyes, but a nod of her head told him that she seemed to accept the idea. She slipped the knife inside her thick brown coat and turned her back. 'Your accent is peculiar,' she said walking away.

'So is yours,' snapped Charlie.

The girl shrugged her shoulders and started rummaging through shelves.

'My name is Charlie.'

The girl threw a glance at Charlie, turned her back and continued rummaging. She pocketed a whole cabbage, a handful of chicken legs, a stick of bread and a chunk of cheese, all squirreled away under her heavy coat.

'And your name is?' Charlie scampered after her. 'What's your name?'

'Belle,' she said finally.

With a pace he could barely keep up with, Charlie shadowed Belle as she snaffled as much food as she could possibly fit into massive sacks, cleverly disguised as coat pockets. Before long, her coat bulged, expanding to double her width. Not another piece of anything could fit into that coat of hers.

After plundering the entire cellar, Belle stopped at a small timber door with slithers of light filtering through tiny gaps either side. She pulled her knife from her coat and slipped it between the door and the frame, carefully placing it under a latch on the other side. From the shadows, Charlie could see the latch lifting. He heard the metal scrape the wood. Belle pushed the door open an inch and stuck her nose against it.

'Maids,' she whispered. 'Do not let them see you.'

'OK,' said Charlie, like he was going to jump out in front of them and wave his arms.

'Your words are strange.' Belle's eyes pierced Charlie's.

You are strange, thought Charlie, his eyes piercing her back. But he didn't say anything this time. He was too scared.

Over the top of Belle's small head, relative to the size of her coat, Charlie stuck his nose against the door. He watched a group of ladies huddled around a long wooden bench, that filled a gigantic kitchen, bigger than his house. In full-length white dresses and matching white caps, they diced carrots on chopping boards.

Thud. Thud. Thud.

Belle lifted her finger to her lips. 'Shoosh!'

She pointed to a small hatch about half way along the kitchen that might have been the entry for a pet.

'We will go through there,' she whispered.

Charlie nodded.

Belle dropped to her knees. She opened the cellar door and squirmed on her stomach across the timber floorboards like a walrus. How she moved at all in that coat, Charlie would never know. He shrugged his shoulders, dropped to his knees and wallowed after her, keeping his head low and his elbows close to his body. As he scrambled under chair legs, Charlie detected pointed shoes bunched together down the other end of the table, just like his. Sharp thuds from the chopping boards barrelled down Charlie's eardrums.

Belle rolled towards a huge timber cupboard with fancy inlays and floral decorations. On the other side of the cupboard was the hatch and above it, a small window. Peering into thick green glass, Charlie detected something odd about the landscape on the other side that worried him. *Really* worried him. It was the colour.

White. Icy-white.

Delicate snowflakes fluttered past the glass and came to rest on a thick wooden pane outside. Charlie shivered.

It's snowing, he thought. *It's June. It never snows in England in June.*

When Belle reached the hatch, she raised an arm and gently twisted a round iron handle. She lifted the hatch. Just big enough to squeeze through, she crawled into the snow. Charlie tailed her. Holding the hatch open with one hand, he wriggled forward. Just as he made it through, a sudden gust of wind blasted though the hatch, causing the doors on the cupboard in the kitchen to fly open. Charlie heard the crockery drop like eggs from the shelves.

Smash. Smash. Smash.

'Run!' screamed Belle.

Jumping to his feet, Charlie sprinted across an icy courtyard after Belle.

Voices exploded behind them.

4

THE FORTRESS

Racing behind Belle, Charlie tackled a maze of white curved walls and terraced gardens with square trimmed hedges. He charged after the dirty girl, in the dirty coat, skidding and slipping in his pointed shoes, which lacked any hint of tread. He caught up with her under a footbridge.

'Do you think they saw us?' Charlie panted.

Belle hunched over, with her hands on her knees, catching her breath.

'I do not know,' she puffed.

Charlie popped his head around the footbridge's thick pylon and somewhat relieved, he couldn't see anyone. He started to focus on the fortress surrounding him. Vast white buildings rose above his head with dusky blue spires on top. Most of the towers, with their steeples and turrets, enclosed a square courtyard in the middle. One tower, much higher than the others, sat in the centre of the courtyard. This tower had a viewing platform under a huge long spire, like a church's steeple, that nearly touched the clouds. Charlie couldn't see anyone up there. On the tip of the spire, a long gold pole extended into the sky with three golden crowns sparkling on top.

'*Where* exactly are we, Belle?' asked Charlie.

'Tre Kronor,' she replied.

Tre Kronor, Charlie thought. *What is Tre Kronor? Or more importantly, where is Tre Kronor?* In that moment he remembered when he arrived in Ancient Greece and was standing in the middle of the courtyard. He recalled the marble buildings and the strange people in their funny robes. Nothing looked familiar. And now here, at Tre Kronor, nothing looked familiar.

Glancing around the vast fortress, Charlie studied the white buildings, the towers and the spires. It looked like a bad version of Disney Land. Then he detected a mammoth wall, made of rocks packed tightly together, that circled the buildings and the adjoining fields — jailing him in. Goosebumps bubbled underneath the surface of his frozen skin.

'Are we in England?' he asked abruptly.

'England,' Belle scoffed. 'We are in Sweden, silly.'

Charlie's heartbeat stopped. He tried not to hyper-ventilate, worried that he might pass out. He consciously tried to breathe slower, so his heart would start up again.

'*Sweden!*' Charlie gasped.

'Stockholm, Sweden.'

Charlie's mind raced. A flash of panic swept over him. *What was he doing in Sweden?* He fumbled his hand under his jacket searching for the Key, and was slightly reassured, when he touched the metal. *At least I can get home*, he thought. Then he started to wonder how he could understand Belle. *Swedish people don't speak English.* Not that he knew of anyway. He rattled his brain for an explanation. He glared at his purple velvet jacket, and his pointed shoes with mauve ribbons, *maybe that's what the Key does?* He thought. *It takes me, the Keyholder, to a different place in time. And I become a person from that place — and a person from that time. That's why I can speak the language. That's why I'm wearing these dumb clothes.*

His mind drifted back to the time he went to Ancient Greece and met Plato. He had never thought about the language before. But it must have happened there as well.

'What date is it?' he said suddenly.

Belle giggled as if Charlie was playing a game with her.

'No seriously, what date is it?' Charlie snapped.

'I do not know dates, but the month is February because the lake is frozen solid.'

'But what year… What year are we in?'

'1650.'

Charlie gasped more air. He tried to breathe normally, but his windpipes were clamping up. He rattled facts in his muddled brain. *I am in Sweden, a thousand miles from home, in the year 1650, with a grubby little girl in a matted coat, trying to find a Frenchman I don't know, who has had his book stolen by a demon. This is seriously insane.*

Belle pointed to a path running alongside one of the trimmed hedges. 'Descartes' apartment is this way. Don't let the Queen's guards see you.'

The Queen's Guards, thought Charlie. *What guards?*

His heart rate quickened with his feet. Icy white snowflakes fell on his eyelashes as his eyes scanned the stone walls, the tower, and the narrow-arched windows. On the high boundary wall enveloping the fortress, two sturdy men paced up and down in long blue coats and triangular hats. Thick long sticks crossed their backs. Charlie squinted. At least he thought they were sticks.

'What are those guards carrying?' Charlie pointed.

'Muskets.'

Muskets, thought Charlie. *What are muskets?*

'Keep your head down,' said Belle. 'They will shoot.'

Yikes. Thought Charlie. *Muskets are guns.*

With his knees trembling, Charlie crept after Belle, taking refuge behind her giant coat. Shuffling along the icy cobblestones, he soon found out what freezing air felt like. At one stage, Charlie put his finger on his nose, it felt like an ice-block. He tried to wriggle his nose, but it didn't move, frozen stiff. Sludge started to seep through his thin socks, causing his ankles to burn. He wished for his boots from home.

Belle knew her way around the castle and, more importantly, around the guards. She guided Charlie along an icy gravel path towards a low gate, at the foot of a tower on the southern corner of the fortress. Unlatching a metal clasp, she led Charlie up two flights of narrow stairs. On a landing at the top, Belle clenched her fist. She thumped on a door that looked way too short.

Whack. Whack.

'Entre,' said a voice in a thick French accent.

Belle shoved the door open as Charlie scuffled in behind her. They entered a cosy sitting room with a pot belly stove burning yellow and red flames in one corner. A knitted blanket lay on a single bed in the opposite corner and a large oak desk rested under a narrow window.

A tubby middle-aged man with long black hair sat at the desk and twitched his horseshoe moustache as they entered. He raised his eyebrows high at the sight of Belle, and raised them even higher at the sight of Charlie.

With the door wide open, a wind flurry whipped off some papers from the desk. It was then that Charlie noticed a razor-sharp scalpel in the man's hand — with a blade that could carve you to pieces.

5

THE CONNECTOR

'Mademoiselle Belle!' The man beamed, wagging the blade in the air. 'You have been missing in action for some time — I have missed my favourite student. How is your family?'

'Hungry.' Belle smiled back at the man. She slammed the door and darted over to the pot belly stove. Frozen solid, Charlie darted after her.

On the way to the stove, Charlie saw a shiny tin bowl resting on top of the desk. As he moved closer, he spied a slimy brain, resembling a fat ball of maggots, sitting in the dish. He stopped dead in his tracks as he gawked at the specimen. Gizzards and muck floated in a jar alongside the bowl. Charlie swallowed hard.

The man's dark eyes peered out from under heavy eyelids that locked with Charlie's. He pointed the scalpel in Charlie's direction. 'I see you have brought me a friend.'

'He was in the cellar,' announced Belle.

Reaching into her giant coat, she plucked out an identical brain and slammed it on the table with a thud. As she did, blood spurted sideways. Charlie nearly gagged.

'Thank you, Mademoiselle!' The man grinned in delight. 'Another fine specimen.'

Belle nodded at the man's pleasure, then spun around and clapped her hands at Charlie. She pointed at the chain. 'Give me the watch.'

Charlie smiled awkwardly at the man. He tugged the chain and the watch dropped from his pocket and dangled. After an awkward long minute of wrangling with the watch's clip, he finally unhooked it from his jacket. Belle grinned and snatched the watch from Charlie's hands. She slipped it carefully into a secret pocket on the inside of her coat. *Not for her own use*, thought Charlie. *She's going to sell it.*

Grinning, Belle tapped her pocket, delighted with her prize.

'Payment,' said Charlie finally, trying to explain himself to the man. 'I asked Belle to bring me here.'

Belle screwed up her button nose. 'His name is Charlie.'

'Monsieur Charlie, delighted to be in your presence.' The man placed the scalpel gently on the table and pushed the dish containing the slimy ball of maggots to one side.

'My name is Descartes.' Over-dramatically, the man bowed his head.

'Err… Hello,' said Charlie, his teeth chattering from the cold. He bowed his head just as dramatically back. He wasn't sure why.

'Please Monsieur, move closer to the stove. I can see you are shivering.'

Quickly, Charlie moved to the pot belly stove and rubbed his rock-hard hands an inch away from the dancing flames. Icicles that had formed on his lashes started to dribble down the sides of his cheeks. Positioning his face closer to the warmth, Charlie tried to defrost his nose.

'And Monsieur, please enlighten me, what brings you to the Queen's Court?'

'Well…'

A pint of blood tore up Charlie's neck and circled it, clamping his throat muscles. He tried to speak, but words didn't come. What should he say to this long-haired Frenchman? His general lack of planning even annoyed him sometimes. He hesitated, trying to think of something plausible to say, but then to his horror Belle spoke for him.

'He was in the cellar, looking for you.' Belle's eyes narrowed and rolled over Charlie. 'Or so he says.'

Descartes' eyebrows lifted. 'Looking for me you say — in the cellar?'

Charlie stepped backwards, away from the stove and wiped his now sweaty palms on his balloon pants. What should he say? He looked at the brain again that Belle had splattered on the desk.

'What do you do with it?' he said suddenly, trying to change the subject. The Frenchmen gave a gentle smile as though he appreciated Charlie's interest.

'He cuts them up,' blurted Belle.

'Please Belle.' The Frenchman dismissed her with a wave of his hand. 'I study the nature of the body.' He paused for a moment. 'And the nature of the mind.'

'How do you mean?' asked Charlie.

'Well, Monsieur — what do we have here?' Descartes poked the maggot ball with the scalpel.

'I'm not exactly sure…' replied Charlie.

'It is a sheep's brain, Monsieur.'

Relieved it wasn't human, Charlie heaved out a bucket of air.

'It is part of a sheep's body. Much like human bodies. Have you ever given any thought to the nature of our bodies?'

'Umm… Not really,' said Charlie.

'Lift up your arm, Monsieur.'

With a large amount of hesitation, Charlie slowly raised his arm.

'Rotate your limb clockwise.'

Belle giggled as Charlie drew air circles with his hand.

Descartes' eyes, shifted from Charlie to the mantel. 'Now, Belle, the clock — bring it to me please.'

She did just as Descartes had instructed, snaffling a tiny box clock from the mantel and then landing it into the Frenchman's palm.

'Your arm works like this clock arm, Monsieur. It is simply a machine. It is physical in nature and physical in substance. Like the mechanics of this clock, with its counterweights and wheels, it can be observed and touched.'

Charlie stopped moving his arm. The air circles had started to hurt his shoulder muscles. He glanced at the clock in the Frenchman's grip and wondered why his arm was being compared to a clock.

'But the mind…' went on Descartes. 'That is of a very different nature.' The Frenchman stood up and tapped his head with his finger. 'Where is your mind, Monsieur?' He lurched around the room as though he was looking for something. 'Can we see it? Can we touch it?'

'It's in my head,' said Charlie. He tapped his skull.
Belle giggled.

'Hmm, but is it?' said Descartes. 'Your mind is your thoughts, your ideas, and your dreams. Your brain is in your head — it is part of the machine of your body, but where are your thoughts? Your ideas? Where are they?' Descartes stuck his head under the desk, under the chair, behind the curtain.

Charlie scratched his scalp.

'Unlike your arm, your mind is not physical in nature. So, can your mind and your body be made of the same substance?' asked the Frenchman.

'Err… I guess not.' Charlie wondered what the point of all this weird discussion was.

'Exactly.' Descartes smiled. 'The body and the mind are indeed different — of a very different nature — yet they talk to each other.'

Descartes shuffled back to the desk and sat down with purpose. He lifted the sparkling scalpel. With the sharp blade, the Frenchman began slicing the brain in half, like he was carving a roast lamb.

Charlie nearly dry-retched. 'So, what are you doing?' he asked.

'I am looking for the place where the mind and body connect,' Descartes said as a matter of fact.

Belle moved closer to the Frenchman and rested her hand on his shoulder. Her green irises glowed as she watched Descartes slice and dice the specimen, clearly delighted to be watching the demonstration.

Picking up one half of the brain, the Frenchman rolled the specimen over in his palm. With the scalpel tip, he pointed to a tiny grey ball in the middle of the brain about the size of a pea.

'See that gland, Monsieur ... that is the *Pineal Gland*. Did you know that, like sheep, we have a Pineal Gland in our brain?'

Charlie stared at the tiny grey lump.

'What does it do?' he asked.

'Indeed Monsieur, what does it do?' Descartes gazed at the tiny grey ball for a few extra-long seconds. Charlie wondered if the Frenchman was asking himself the same question.

'It is the connector.' Descartes tapped the gland with the tip of the scalpel. 'It is the very place where our mind connects with our body.'

The Frenchman's brown eyes sparkled as he poked the little grey ball again. 'The mind talks to our body, through the Pineal Gland. The connector is the seat of our soul.'

'But how does it do that?' asked Charlie. 'How does our mind talk to our body?'

'See these ventricles attached to the gland.' Descartes poked a set of tiny arteries expanding outwards from the pea-sized ball.

'Yeah,' said Charlie.

'Like a very subtle wind, or rather, like a pure and lively flame, animal spirits come down these ventricles and talk to the body,' said Descartes.

Charlie examined the pea ball. He had never heard of the Pineal Gland before, or any gland for that matter that connected the body with the mind.

The Frenchman's eyes rolled over the murky specimen.

'Our mind, our ideas, our thoughts, our dreams, even our soul — they are all one, you know. They are all of the same nature and substance. The body however, is of a very different nature and substance to the mind.'

With scalpel in hand, Descartes abruptly stood up. His eyes widened and focussed on Charlie. He lunged forward, brandishing the weapon an inch from Charlie's face. Descartes' dark pupils dilated. Belle sprung into position behind the Frenchman.

Charlie jolted backwards. His leather pointers scuffled across a Persian rug. The Frenchman grabbed the collar of his jacket.

'Now tell me,' said Descartes in a firm voice. The scalpel hovering at the end of Charlie's nose. 'Why are *you* here?'

6

THE THREE DREAMS

Charlie's heartbeat raced.

'I… I heard you were in trouble,' he stuttered. 'I… um… I have come to help you.'

With narrow eyes, Descartes stared at Charlie.

'Trouble,' he snapped. 'What kind of trouble?'

'Your book,' blurted Charlie. 'I am here about your book.'

'It is him!' shouted Belle.

'Quiet, Belle!' Descartes threw the girl an angry look.

'Who?' barked Charlie.

'Tell us what you know about my manuscript,' said Descartes.

'Err… Nothing… Except that it was stolen.'

'It is him!' shouted Belle again.

'Quiet, Belle. Please!' growled Descartes. 'Who are you? Who sent you here?'

Charlie ruffled the lace on his long sleeve cuffs as he met the Frenchman's gaze. His head almost exploded. He thought about running, but his legs didn't budge. It was like his shoes were glued to the floorboards.

Should I tell Descartes the real story? Should I tell him how it all began? How I travelled through time and wound up in Ancient Greece? Should I tell him about Plato and the Oracle, and the Eternal Key? And how the Key started smoking this morning and it took me to Ted. Or even how I ended up here?

Charlie decided to say nothing about any of that. It would freak Descartes out.

Looking for reassurance, Charlie tapped his pocket with his fingers, feeling for the security of the Key. A glimpse of Ted's face flashed in his mind. An air of calmness swept over him, as if Ted was there, in the room with him. He drew in a big breath of air.

'Descartes, I am here to help you,' said Charlie. 'I am here to find your book and return it to you. You just have to trust me.'

As he said it, Charlie didn't even know if he could help the Frenchman or not. If he was honest, he had no real clue what he was doing there at all — stuck with two weirdos, in a weird place, in a weird time.

He felt so far out of his depth, he just wanted to go home.

'We cannot trust him,' snorted Belle. 'He could be the demon.'

'Demon?' Charlie remembered what Ted had said about the demon. 'What demon?'

Descartes' large brown eyes reduced to slits. He glared at Charlie as he plucked at a tuft of black hair jutting out from underneath his bottom lip. After a long minute of awkward silence, Descartes' eyes glazed over and frown lines emerged on his forehead as if a painful memory was resurfacing. Charlie could see the Frenchman was thinking about something else.

Descartes' eyes suddenly widened. 'He cannot be the demon.'

'Why not?' said Belle, almost disappointed.

'Because the demon is in my mind…' The Frenchman hobbled back to the desk and slumped into the worn leather chair. He pointed to a smaller parlour chair sitting under the window and motioned to Charlie to sit. 'Please, Monsieur.'

Belle moved behind Descartes.

'Indeed Monsieur, my manuscript was stolen,' said Descartes so quietly that Charlie almost didn't hear him.

'Stolen.' Charlie scraped the liquorice shaped legs of the chair across the floorboards, closer to

Descartes. 'When was it stolen?'

'I must start at the beginning, Monsieur.' Descartes' eyes went glassy, his lips quivered, his emotions not far from the surface.

'Monsieur, when I was a young man, in my twenties, I had three dreams — the strangest set of dreams.'

Charlie studied the wrinkles around the Frenchman's eyes. He tried to guess how old he was. *He must be at least fifty now*, he thought.

'In my first dream, I was sitting in a room curled up in my armchair, next to a big earthenware stove.' Descartes nodded towards the pot belly stove. 'Just like that one.'

Charlie eyeballed the stove and shivered. He wished he was closer to it.

'The dream was so real, I felt the warmth from the stove on my face, even as I was dreaming. Yet there was no fire lit in the room.'

'So, you could feel the heat, but the fire wasn't burning,' said Charlie.

'That is right, Monsieur. Then, in the same dream, I was walking down the street and ghosts appeared in front of me.'

'Ghosts,' whispered Charlie. His heart fluttered.

'Ghosts,' repeated Descartes. 'Terrified, I started to run away from them, but I couldn't move my right side, like I had a stroke, so I hobbled along in a grotesque position.'

Belle nodded her head, as though she had heard this story before.

'Anyway, the wind picked up, and started spinning me around.'

'Did the ghosts get you?' asked Charlie.

Descartes shook his head. 'No. I saw a church. The door was open. But before I could take refuge, a man appears in the garden asking me to carry a melon for him.'

'A melon,' said Charlie. 'That's really weird.'

Descartes nodded. 'I continued walking, dragging my body along, carrying the melon. But everyone else was walking normally. I was so unhappy. I woke up… and thought there was evil in that dream.'

'What a weird dream,' said Charlie.

'It was,' nodded Descartes. 'After two hours of unhappy thoughts I went back to sleep. But then I have a second dream. This time I hear a thunderous explosion. Sparks fly around me, so bright I can see objects in my bedroom. I wake up again.'

'So, you dreamt you heard the loud explosion?' asked Charlie.

'Yes,' said Descartes. 'The explosion was in my dreams.'

Descartes' eyes glazed over. He stared outside the window.

'But Monsieur, I had a third dream. And it was

this dream that is the most troubling.'

Biting his lower lip, Descartes' eyebrows twitched, as if he was trying to compose himself. Tears welled in the Frenchman's eyes and Charlie could see that his emotions were spilling over.

'In front of me on a table was a book, a book with poems in it. I flick through the book and immediately find a poem called *Which path in life will I choose?* Then a man appears in front of me. He is not known to me. He starts reciting a poem called, *What is and what is not?* He tells me the poem he is reciting is in the poetry book. But I skim the pages and I can't find the poem. Then the man disappears.' Descartes' voice quivered. 'I was troubled by this third dream Monsieur. I took it as a sign. God was trying to tell me something.'

'Tell you what?' asked Charlie.

'What indeed?' Descartes' glassy eyes left the window and became fixated on Charlie. He leaned forward. His facial expression intense.

'Do you sometimes think your dreams are so vivid they must be real? Only to find later that you had been asleep?'

'Yes,' replied Charlie. 'It happens to me all the time. It's really scary.'

'Exactly… and so Monsieur, I started thinking about these dreams. I thought about feeling the warmth from the stove on my face. I thought about hearing the loud explosion. I thought about everything in those dreams. And I realised that I couldn't tell the difference between being awake and asleep. I couldn't tell the difference because all the information that comes to me, when I am both asleep and awake, comes from my senses — my eyes, my ears, touch and so on. I realised something important, Monsieur. My senses don't tell me what is really happening.'

'How do you mean?'

'Everything that I saw, everything I heard, everything I felt. Every bit of information that came to me in those dreams came from my senses — none of it happened. They were just dreams. And so how did I know they were just dreams?'

'I don't know,' replied Charlie. 'How did you know?'

'My mind,' Descartes tapped his forehead with his finger. 'My mind knew they were dreams, but my senses did not. My senses could not be trusted.'

Charlie moved uncomfortably in the chair.

'The senses deceive us. They don't speak the truth. We can never rely on them. Our mind is far more reliable.' Descartes dwelled. 'And so, it occurred to me that all the knowledge I had gained over the years had been gathered by my senses. Everything I knew — none of it could be relied upon. I had built a house on unstable foundations. This revelation changed the course of my work. I knew that everything I had learned now had to be doubted.'

'But I don't understand,' said Charlie. 'What has any of this got to do with your stolen book?'

'Tell him,' snapped Belle.

'I had the third dream again, just a week ago. But this time it was different.'

'Different,' said Charlie. 'How?'

'The man appears once more,' Descartes went on. 'He pulls out the poetry book from his back pocket and he changes form. I could have sworn he was turning from man to skeleton, then back again.'

Descartes' face appeared frightened, as though he was recalling the image he saw as he spoke. 'But the worse thing about it all, he didn't recite the poem. He just kept on asking the same question over and over again. *What is and what is not? What is and what is not? What is and what is not?*'

Descartes started to choke up.

'The skeleton peered down at me with menacing eyes and said, *Are they your thoughts, or a demon's?* Then with a horrid gut-wrenching laugh, he vanished with the poetry book.'

The Frenchman wiped his eyes with the tip of a handkerchief as Belle placed a gentle hand on his shoulder.

'And when I woke up.' Descartes sniffed. 'The manuscript I had been working on for many years —

Meditations, my life's work… was gone.'

'But what did he mean, *Are they your thoughts or a demon's*?' asked Charlie.

'Well that is just it, Monsieur… Have you ever thought about thinking?'

'Err…'

'Have you ever thought about your own thoughts and where they come from?'

'Um, no… Not really,' said Charlie.

'Think about this… Is it possible your thoughts are not your own thoughts at all? You think you are thinking — but someone else has done the thinking for you. Maybe someone is sitting up there somewhere in a little control room, putting thoughts in your head. So really you have no thoughts at all. They are all someone else's thoughts. And if you have no thoughts at all — who are you? What are you? If you cannot think for yourself — you cannot possibly exist. You are merely someone else's puppet on a string.'

'I can't say I've ever thought about that,' said Charlie.

'Well, Monsieur, I think about someone else controlling my thoughts every single day that I breathe.'

'But how could that happen?' asked Charlie.

Descartes raised his finger. 'Look at the dreams, how do they happen? Who knows what is real and what is not?'

The Frenchman sniffed. His hands trembled.

'My biggest fear might be true,' said Descartes. 'My thoughts are not my thoughts at all – they are the thoughts of a demon, who has taken over my mind.'

'I don't know anything about demons,' said Charlie. 'All I know is that I have to get your book back.'

'But you cannot,' said Descartes. 'I fear the demon is my mind — with my book — impossible to catch.'

Charlie eyed the sheep's brain sliced in half, sitting in the tin dish on the desk. He examined the Pineal Gland and recalled Ted's words. 'And remember, the Key can take you anywhere.'

Suddenly, Charlie realised what he needed to do. He had to somehow get into Descartes' mind. *But a mind is nothing.* He thought. *It's not even a place.* He stared at the tiny grey pea in the middle of the sliced brain. *It's the connector. It's where the body connects with the mind. If I can get to Descartes' Pineal Gland, I can enter his mind.*

'Not impossible to catch,' said Charlie with confidence.

In a flash, Charlie pulled the Key from his jacket. 'I know how to get your book back.'

'A weapon!' Belle screamed.

She pounced on top of Charlie, crash-tackling

him to the floor.

'It's not a weapon, it's a Key!' shrieked Charlie. 'It won't hurt you!'

'He is the demon!' Belle clawed her fingernails at the Key.

'I'm not a freakin' demon!'

The pair brawled like tigers on the Persian rug.

'Let go!' yelled Charlie. 'I know what I'm doing!'

'Demon!' screeched Belle.

She gripped her hands around the Key, crushing Charlie's finger knuckles.

'The Key can take me anywhere,' shouted Charlie. 'I'm going to the Pineal Gland!'

'No!' cried Belle. *No!'*

Boom.

A flash of light blasted from the Key, and shot up Charlie's arm, just like the electric current from the lightning strike. His body shuddered with the explosion.

The Key started spinning on the rug, faster and faster — with Charlie attached to it, and Belle attached to him.

Charlie tried to peel his fingers from the Key, but they were bonded to the gold like cement.

'Whoa!'

The skin on Charlie's face distorted and shook unnaturally. His teeth clanged like chimes. Turning wildly, he gulped for air.

His body swivelled with Belle's, until the pair became a giant blur. Spinning. Spinning. They vanished into a cloud of dust.

7

THE ANIMAL SPIRITS

Thud.

Charlie landed on something spongy and moist. Rubbing his eyes, Charlie glimpsed a lump of a person beside him. Belle lay on her back, sprawled out like a dead chicken in her brown coat. She massaged a bulge on her forehead.

'What just happened?' she whispered.

'I'm not exactly sure.' Charlie staggered uneasily to his feet. Whatever he was standing on felt squishy and uneven.

With its faint orange glow, Charlie spied the Key on a slippery red mound. He sprang over to it and scooped it up. Using the Key as a torch, he flashed it upwards. Above his head hung a massive dome, almost transparent, and suspended by large hollow tubes. Round, concave walls, displayed bright red arteries that looked like rat tracks across a slimy grey film. The whiff of raw flesh hung in the air, as Charlie gazed at the huge balloon-like chamber surrounding him.

'Where are we?' Belle's wide eyes scrutinised the gooey folds of flesh.

'You should have let go,' barked Charlie. He shuffled over to a wet pink wall and strained one ear. He heard a gushing sound like water travelling through pipes.

Belle stumbled to her feet and pricked up her ears. 'What is that *noise*?'

'Blood pumping,' replied Charlie.

'Blood pumping,' repeated Belle. 'What do you mean blood pumping?'

'We are in Descartes' head,' said Charlie. 'In his Pineal Gland.'

'You are a fool.' Belle snarled.

'No seriously, we're in Descartes' Pineal Gland — the Key has brought us here.'

Belle glared at Charlie and the Key glowing in his hand.

Charlie ran a finger across the slimy walls. 'We have to find the connection.'

'A connection to what?'

'Descartes' mind.'

'You really *are* mad.'

'It's the only way to get the book back. We have to leave his body and get into his mind — get into his thoughts.' Charlie patted the fleshy walls, as the Key flashed.

In her heavy coat, Belle stumbled to her feet and staggered towards Charlie. Her eyes studied the walls. After a moment, she stretched out an arm and pressed her hand against the slippery grey matter.

'Eek!' Feeling the gooey slime, she quickly pulled her palm away. Seconds later, she lifted a finger into the air and traced a shape on the wall without touching it.

'It's a blood cell — a huge blood cell,' Belle gasped.

'Told you — we're in Descartes' Pineal Gland,' said Charlie.

'But we cannot be,' Belle snapped. 'We cannot be standing in Descartes' apartment one moment, and standing inside his brain the next.'

'I can,' said Charlie, running his hands along the walls trying to find a way out. 'The Key can take me anywhere. But *you* shouldn't be here — *you* should have let go.'

Belle plopped her cold dirty hands on her hips. 'Well if the Key brought us here, it can get us out of here — give it to me!'

She snatched the Key from Charlie's grip and

waved it violently in the air.

'It won't work for you,' said Charlie. 'You're not the *Keyholder.*'

After about a minute of flapping the Key around, Belle roared with frustration and tossed it at one of the blood pumping veins. She slumped onto a chunk of red slimy flesh with her head in her hands.

Charlie swooped on the Key.

'It's alright,' he said. 'There must be a connector somewhere.'

He eyed a gland that was an odd leaf-like shape and a deeper grey than the others. On closer inspection it looked thicker and it connected to a whole lot of smaller veins as if it might be the mother vein, feeding the babies. He pressed it hard with his palm. A breeze raced down the tube. 'Come here, Belle — help me push!'

'Why?' she snarled.

'I think it's the connector.'

Reluctantly, she stood up on the blood vessels and bounced her way back towards Charlie. She positioned her body alongside his and started to push hard.

In a matter of seconds, the ventricles began to inflate like swollen tubes. Charlie felt a subtle wind drift down from the shafts. Like they had set a domino display in motion, the small threads on the tips of the arteries started to stretch and join one another, and the valves pulled together and opened allowing the airstream to gather pace.

Next, Charlie heard an onslaught of roars, rumbling down the hollow tubes. Sounds of tigers, lions and bears ripping at each other's throats. A cyclone whipped up the roaring sirens, that rattled and crashed, causing the body pipes to convulse.

'Animal spirits,' whispered Belle, watching the chain of motions. 'Descartes calls them animal spirits.'

The roars became louder. The pipes pulsed faster. Charlie threw his hands to his ears to shut out the noise. But the main ventricle opened, slimy looking skin left the walls and enveloped Charlie and Belle together. In an instant the tube swallowed them whole.

8

THE CABINETS

Spat out by an artery, Charlie and Belle tumbled together on what felt like a hard-concrete floor.

Slowly, Charlie rose to his feet. Either side of him stood white glossy cabinets, the size of sports lockers, each with a metal handle. Rows and rows of them, which seemed to go on forever. In between each locker was a narrow gap, barely big enough to squeeze through.

'What is this place?' Belle wiped sludge from her coat.

'I have no clue.' Charlie did the same. Muck dribbled from his balloon pants.

They both walked up and down the rows of cabinets, trying to get their bearings.

Eventually, Charlie sucked in his stomach. 'I'm going through here.'

He rammed himself between two lockers. Belle squished in behind him and nearly got stuck in her food-packed coat.

On the other side of the cabinets was another row of cabinets. And behind them, more cabinets. And more cabinets. Charlie snaked faster between the cabinets. He couldn't see the end of any row; it was like the lockers went on for eternity.

Charlie inched towards one of the lockers and stretched out his hand ready to pull the metal knob. But just as he did, he saw a light bulb on top. He thought better of touching the handle and quickly pulled his hand away. Now focusing on the knob, he spotted a small hand-written label stuck to the cabinet neatly above it.

'Look at this,' he said. 'It says *Mathematics, Algebra* — with an equation underneath.'

Belle moved to the cabinet next to Charlie. 'This one says *Mathematics, Algebra* too.' Belle's eyes flicked from the locker in front of Charlie to the locker in front of her. 'But this one has a different equation.'

Charlie moved faster along the rows. 'It looks like every possible combination of every mathematical equation is in here.'

After passing at least fifty cabinets, Charlie decided to change rows.

'These labels over here say *Mathematics, Geometry*.' Charlie studied the equation underneath. Even with his limited math knowledge, he knew exactly what the equation was.

'This one is the formula to find the angle of a triangle,' he said.

'That is funny,' said Belle. 'Descartes loves Mathematics — he spends hours doing calculations on the angles of triangles.'

Charlie and Belle locked eyes for a second too long.

'It actually worked.' Charlie's eyes widened.

'What has worked?' said Belle.

'We're in his mind,' said Charlie. 'We are in Descartes' mind.'

'How do you know that?' Belle puffed. 'Who would have cabinets in their mind?' Her eyes scanned the surrounds. 'Hundreds and hundreds of them.'

'Maybe each cabinet is a thought,' said Charlie. 'When he thinks about something — he opens a cabinet.'

'Well…' said Belle. 'Descartes always said that the mind was separate from the body, and made of a different substance, but I never imagined it would look like this.'

Charlie shrugged his shoulders.

Skipping across a number of rows of cabinets, Charlie noticed that the topics started to change away from mathematics. *Ideas, Philosophy, the Universe,* and *Ideas, Philosophy, Dreams.*

Charlie began to wonder what his mind would look like. Could it really look like this, just thousands and thousands of thoughts stored into filing cabinets? All lined up one after the other with neat little labels. He became convinced his mind didn't look like this one.

Firstly, he didn't have this many thoughts. Secondly, his thoughts would be all over the place, in no particular order. Scattered randomly. Some of his labels wouldn't even make sense. Charlie imagined the labels on his math cabinets. Half of the equations would be wrong.

'Look!' Belle pointed her finger. 'That light over there on that cabinet – it is twinkling green!'

Charlie's eyeballs darted to where Belle was pointing. A lightbulb flashing green sparkled on top of a cabinet at least ten rows from where he was standing.

'C'mon!' Charlie shouted.

Like moths, Charlie and Belle dashed towards the flickering globe.

Stopping dead in front of the cabinet, Charlie watched the globe for a minute. A current flowed inside the bulb that looked like some kind of strange green liquid. With every moment passing, the globe was getting brighter and brighter.

'What does the label say?' said Belle. She peered over Charlie's shoulder. 'Can you read it?'

'*Ideas, Philosophy, Demon* — it must be the cabinet with Descartes' thoughts on the demon.' Charlie glanced at Belle. 'Shall we open it?'

'No,' she snapped.

'We have to,' said Charlie. 'We don't have a choice.'

'You open it,' said Belle.

Taking a tentative step forward, Charlie slowly extended his trembling fingers towards the knob.

'Be careful!' barked Belle, unhelpfully.

Charlie felt the cold metal underneath his fingertips. He extended his hand further, and wrapped all of his fingers around the knob, tightening his grip.

'Pull it!' said Belle, the suspense unbearable.

Charlie felt the muscles in his wrist stiffen. His upper biceps tensed. Sweat dribbled from his forehead and he bit his lip. He leaned his body into the cabinet and tugged hard at the knob.

In that second, the flashing bulb smashed and the locker door flung open like a refrigerator. With it came an explosion of white light. Blinded, Charlie and Belle tried to step back, but they got sucked into the cabinet by a windstorm of air. Green slime oozed from the broken glass down to the metal knob, then the door slammed shut.

9

THE BLACK RAVEN

Charlie lay on his back and squinted at the beam of sunlight glistening on the oversized watchtower of Tre Kronor Castle. Stumbling to his feet, he brushed ice flakes from his velvet balloon pants.

Belle rubbed her eye sockets as she hobbled to a standing position. She spied two guards on the boundary wall in the distance, pacing up and down with their long muskets. Quickly, she ducked into the shadows of the footbridge and pulled Charlie with her.

'Why are we back here at Tre Kronor?' asked Belle.

'We must be in one of Descartes' thoughts,' said

Charlie. 'He must be thinking about Tre Kronor.'

Charlie remembered the cabinet, the knob and the label that read, *Ideas, Philosophy, Demon.*

'The demon must be here somewhere as well,' he said. 'With the book.'

'How can you be so sure?'

Charlie wasn't sure of anything anymore.

'It must be here,' he whispered.

Belle shook her head sideways, as though she didn't understand anything that was going on. 'What do we do now? Look for a demon?'

'Yep,' said Charlie. His eyes skimmed across the fortress and stopped on the tip of the spire on the central watchtower. On the end of the pole, nestled in the three golden crowns, sat a huge black bird.

Charlie watched the creature lurch upright and span its menacing wings. The long wedge-shaped tail whipped the spiked points of the golden crowns. It squawked and squawked, like it had something stuck in its shaggy feathered throat. Beady yellow eyes glared at Charlie and Belle. Beating wings thrashed the air, hinting that the bird might be a predator ready to strike.

'That bird.' Hairs on the back of Charlie's neck spiked upwards. 'What's it doing?'

Belle squinted at the golden crowns. 'It is a raven. A black raven… A big one.'

Watching the scavenger closely, Charlie saw it

launch from the three crowns and soar towards the sun, its shimmering black body reflecting like a mirror. As the bird soared higher, it flapped its massive wings. The sounds thundered across the sky. Suddenly, the bird changed direction. Piercing yellow eyes became fixated on Charlie — a creature possessed.

The raven swooped.

'It's coming for me!' screamed Charlie.

Throwing his hands over his head, he ducked for cover. But hefty wings thumped his face, driving him into the ice.

'Shoo!' yelled Belle.

She waved her arms frantically and tried to kick the enormous bird off Charlie, its prey. Stolen bread and cheese tumbled from her coat pockets and rolled like marbles across the snow.

But the raven wasn't scared off. It wasn't going anywhere.

The bird shrilled out squawks that rattled the forest beyond the fortress. With an upright tail, and beating wings, it charged Charlie, tossing him into the snow. The Key dropped from Charlie's jacket and bounced along the ice.

'Shoo! Shoo!' Belle shook her fist violently.

Charlie lunged at the Key with his frozen stiff fingers. Razor-sharp claws drilled holes in his hand like nails.

'Aaargh!' Charlie yelled.

The raven seized the Key between its giant claws and launched into the sky, shooting toward the sun.

'Come back!' screeched Charlie. 'That Key is mine!'

With a final piercing squawk, the raven spiralled skyward, catching an explosion of wind, and disappeared with the Key into the painful glare of the sun.

10

THE RUSTY SIGN

'We have to go after it,' snapped Charlie.

He sprung from the snow, clutching his bloodied hand. He darted under the footbridge, racing along a gravel path that bordered a thick high hedge, in the direction of the bird. Belle ripped after him.

Sprinting away from the main buildings of the fortress, Charlie jumped a field fence and crossed a frosty paddock. The raven zoomed towards a large timber barn, with a second-floor loft and a high-pitched roof. Charlie tracked the bird through the barn's alley gate and towards some empty horse stalls at the rear.

Soaring higher now, the bird flew into the dusty

rafters supporting the pitched roof. Chasing down the bird, Charlie scrambled up a ladder to the loft. Trying desperately to keep up, Belle pummelled the ladder rungs behind him.

Standing knee-deep in hay, Charlie spotted the creature settling on an old rusty sign that hung from two chains in the roof's rafters. Scrawled onto the metal plate, in old style writing, Charlie read the words: WHICH PATH SHOULD I CHOOSE?

'What does it mean?' whispered Belle. She frowned at the sign, then at the yellow irises of the black raven perched on top of it.

'Who knows?' said Charlie.

Groans from the rusty metal grating on the chains rattled across the breeze. Charlie stepped forward towards the raven. The Key flashed in its claws.

Just as Charlie moved, the bird launched from the sign, wailed out an almighty screech, and tore across the loft's rafters, swooping back down to the horse stalls, and out the alley gate. The blustery gale from the creature's wings caused the loft ladder to plummet and snap into shards in the hay below.

'The bird is gone,' said Belle, stating the obvious.

'I know,' whispered Charlie. 'So is the ladder.'

They both glared at the snapped bits of timber, twenty feet below.

'We are stuck up here now,' said Belle, stating the obvious again.

Charlie re-read the sign. 'Which path should I choose?'

'Look!' Charlie pointed to one side of the loft. On a single track stood a small cart attached to a thick rope, that hung from some kind of wheeled pulley system.

Noticing Charlie's interest in the pulley, Belle said, 'It is a treadwheel.'

Charlie tugged at the rope hanging from the pulley, and the barn cart started to move forward along the track. He kept on pulling and noticed a square timber flap at the end of the barn was lifting from the wall. The motion created a large hole in the wall.

Curious to see how the system worked, Charlie crawled towards the flap.

'What's it for?' he said.

'Grain,' replied Belle. 'The trolley tips at the hole and grain drops in the pens outside.'

As Charlie opened the flap, he noticed weird pictures etched into the timber. The first image seemed to be a pair of round eyeballs, each drawn with a pupil, an iris and with thick lines as veins. A second picture was equally detailed, a long straight nose with side shadow lines and a rose beneath the nostrils. The third sketch was an ear, the fourth a finger. Charlie couldn't make out the last one. It just looked like a blob.

Charlie lifted the flap, stuck his head through the hole and saw a large haystack in a pen below. Beyond the pen was a path, lined by a high stone fence, that seemed to disappear over a hill.

'There's a haystack in this pen,' he yelled. 'And a path that goes towards a hill.'

Belle pointed to another trolley on the opposite side of the loft. 'There is another grain trolley over there.' She scuffled across the hay towards it.

Charlie turned his focus to Belle opposite.

'What's outside over there?' he shouted.

Opening the flap on the wall and poking her head out, she shouted back. 'Another path.'

'Where does that one go?' said Charlie.

'Take a look.'

Charlie made his way across the thick straw, that spiked like long needles into his thin socks. Kneeling down in front of the flap, Charlie saw no pictures, no writing, nothing. It was completely blank.

'What is it?' whispered Belle. She could see that Charlie was frowning.

'The other flap has pictures,' said Charlie. He lifted the flap and stuck out his head. Outside he spied another pen below, only this one was crammed full with muddy pigs. Beyond the pen was another path, also lined with a high stone wall, but this path led towards a dense dark forest.

Belle stared at the blank piece of wood. 'So which

path do we choose?'

'I have no idea,' said Charlie. He slammed the flap shut.

Just as he did, the timber beams on the roof started to rumble. The floorboards under their feet began to quiver. A mound of straw rose in the middle of the loft. Then a large object burst through the hay. Right in front of them, stood a giant wax candle. Bigger than a water tank, it grew larger and higher by the second — as if it was alive.

11

THE BEESWAX

Charlie and Belle crouched in the hay trembling at the sight of the ever-expanding candle. Terrified, they watched the wick hit one of the rafters. Then the candle stopped growing and just sat there.

'Why is it here?' Charlie's breath quickened. His eyes rolled over the huge chunk of wax.

'We should get out of here,' growled Belle. She dashed towards where the ladder had been, but she had forgotten it was snapped into pieces. Balancing on the edge of the loft on her toes, she examined the horse stalls below.

'It's too high,' said Charlie. 'You'll break your neck.'

He crept towards the supersized candle.

'We must leave,' insisted Belle, still balancing on the loft's edge.

'We can't go anywhere,' Charlie whispered. 'Until we've chosen a path.'

He circled the candle. As he did, he remembered Ted's words, *Follow the path of truth.*

Studying the candle, Charlie noticed the colour, a deep yellow, almost mustard-like. It was different from the candles his mum had at home.

'What do you think it's made of?' he asked.

'Beeswax,' said Belle. She moved slowly towards the candle. 'It is from the hives. You cut it out to get to the honey.'

Charlie inched forward. He wanted to touch it. With a large amount of hesitation, he tapped the wax with his fingernail. It made a strange hollow sound. But within seconds of touching it, the wick on top of the candle ignited into a flame. Burning a dazzling yellow, the flame danced across the top of the wax. It released an unusual sweet scent, like melted toffee.

But then the candle started to extend higher. The wick soared beyond the loft's rafters towards the hatched straw roof. A violent wind-drift blasted upwards, and the straw ignited.

The flames began to spread in the hay above the timber beams. Thick black smoke filled a corner of the loft.

'The roof is burning!' cried Belle.

'We have to choose a path behind one of those flaps,' barked Charlie. 'But which one?'

Charlie raced over to the flap with the pictures. He turned his head back towards the candle. 'The answer is here somewhere, in Descartes' mind.'

'Or the demon's mind,' coughed Belle. 'Who is trying to burn us alive.'

Charlie focused his attention on Belle. 'You're Descartes' student. You have watched him work. Does he do anything with candles?'

'No!' snapped Belle. 'He just works under their light — that is all.'

The flames extended from the thatch roof to the thick timber rafters. Blackened ash spiralled from the building's rickety frame and landed in Charlie's hair. The temperature in the loft soared. The space was so hot the giant candle began to melt. Hot liquid gushed from the wick, spilling down the sides of the candle's massive form. A puddle of wax started to pool at the base and flowed steadily outwards across the floorboards.

'Think Belle!' yelled Charlie. 'Think!'

Spreading quickly now, the melted wax oozed towards Charlie's pointed shoes.

'Wait a minute,' said Belle. 'Descartes did do something weird one day.'

'What?' screamed Charlie. 'What did he do?'

A piece of straw landed on Charlie's head and

singed his hair. He battered it down with his bare hands.

'He gave me a candle. He told me to look at it, smell it, he even told me to taste it. But I did not bite it. That would be silly. He told me to roll it around in my hands.'

'Hurry Belle.' Charlie's feet dodged the pool of wax moving towards him.

'Then he asked me to take it over to the stove — so I did.'

'What happened then?' barked Charlie.

'It melted.'

'It melted?'

'Yes… and…'

'And what, Belle? Hurry!'

'Well… He asked me to study it again.'

The hot wax touched the tip of Charlie's leather shoe. He felt the intense heat on his big toe. He gritted his teeth. 'You're not making any sense.'

'Look at the wax!' she shouted over the crackling flames. Beads of sweat poured down her grimy face, leaving shiny track marks on her cheeks. 'That is what Descartes wanted me to do. Look at the wax.'

'It's melting!' snapped Charlie.

'Yes. It looks nothing like it did before. It smells different, it feels different.' She kicked the puddle of wax at her feet. 'Strike it with your hand, it would sound different. If your tongue could stand the heat, it would taste different. Everything about the wax is different.'

'But what is his point?'

'Descartes' point is…' She raised a finger into the air like some crazy professor. 'It is the same piece of wax!'

'We know that,' yelled Charlie. 'We saw it melt!'

'Ah… But that's exactly Descartes' point. Everything you know about the wax, before it melted, came from your eyes, your ears, your nose, your taste buds and even your fingers. But now your senses are telling you something else. Nothing is the same. The wax has completely changed.'

'I'm not following!' Charlie slapped a piece of burning straw from his purple jacket in frustration.

'How do we know it is the same piece of wax?' Belle said, as if she was pondering life and had all the time in the world. 'If you relied on your senses, you would say it was not the same piece of wax — every part of the wax is different. But your mind is telling you something else. Your mind tells you it is the same piece of wax. It understands the wax better than your senses do. Descartes says your mind is more reliable. Trust your mind he says, not your senses — he calls this *reason*.'

Charlie eyeballed the boiling pool of wax about to bubble into his ugly leather shoes. Then, a switch came on in his brain.

'Those pictures on that flap.' Charlie pointed to the timber flap with the etchings.

'What about them?' said Belle.

'They are the senses — eyes, nose, ear, finger.' Charlie gasped. 'The blob. It's a tongue — taste! C'mon' get in this trolley. We choose this path.' He dashed towards the cart near the flap without etchings.

'Why?' Belle hesitated.

'We do as Descartes said, we don't trust the senses,' snapped Charlie. 'This one doesn't have any senses on it — it's blank, we trust the mind.'

'I prefer the other cart,' growled Belle. 'It has a haystack underneath it.'

Muddy pigs squealed from the pen below.

'Get in!' shouted Charlie.

Belle jumped in the trolley with Charlie.

'We trust the mind!' he screamed.

Charlie tugged at the rope. The flap flung open. The trolley tipped forward. Falling like two potato sacks, the pair plunged from the loft.

Boom.

The trolley on the opposite side of the loft exploded into flames.

Belle smacked face-first into the mud. Charlie landed on the back of an unsuspecting pig. Shrieks from the hog rang across the pen.

12

THE FOREST

Surrounded by monster trees, higher than skyscrapers, Charlie and Belle meandered along a path sprinkled with snow. Charlie could tell the forest was ancient by the deep moss that stretched up the knotted trunks and strangled new growth. The wide thick canopy overhead, together with a setting sun, made sure darkness came from all sides. Smells of damp earth and rotting roots drifted down the gully behind them. With every step deeper into the wood the path narrowed until it was almost impossible to see any path at all.

'Have you been in this forest before?' Charlie asked. He picked a chunk of mud off his jacket from the pigpen.

'No,' said Belle. 'They tell you at Tre Kronor to stay away from it.'

'Why is that?' asked Charlie. He wasn't sure he wanted to hear the answer.

'People have entered the wood — but they never come out again.'

'Great,' said Charlie. He flicked the mud onto the path with two fingers.

Kraaw. Kraaw.

Short, high pitched blasts came from a hidden creature, high in the tree tops. But rustling leaves and falling twigs confirmed the bird's presence. Charlie knew it was the raven with the Key, tailing them, watching their every move.

Charlie took slow and careful steps. Thick leafy undergrowth made sure you had no clue what you were stepping on. *Snakes and spiders would live here for sure*, he thought. He pulled his white stocking socks up to his knees, knowing that the protection from the paper-thin material would be useless from a pair of fangs. He gulped.

Sob. Sob.

Charlie stopped in his tracks. He turned his head and saw Belle sitting on a fallen branch, her face in her hands, crying.

'Are you alright?' he asked.

'No,' she sobbed. 'I am not alright.'

Charlie went over to Belle and sat next to her on

the log. He watched her pull a dirty cloth from her coat pocket and blow her nose.

'We will be OK,' he whispered. 'I promise you.'

He suddenly felt guilty. He knew he couldn't promise anything. He watched her tears roll down her cheeks, and the grime under her eyes smudge. *She looks exhausted*, he thought. *I have caused all of this. I have brought her here, to this creepy place, just so I can find a stupid book.*

'Why are we here?' she said.

Charlie sucked in a truckload of icy cold air.

'Why have you brought me here?' said Belle again. Her voice louder and more determined. 'Where did you come from?'

'Listen, Belle,' Charlie whispered. 'I'm not from around here.'

'Where then? Where are you from?'

Charlie hesitated for a moment. 'I'm not from your country — or from your time.'

Belle jumped up, her piercing green eyes shooting daggers at Charlie.

'From what country are you from? And what time?'

Charlie wished he could explain himself to her, but he couldn't. He just couldn't. He couldn't explain anything.

'It's not important,' he said.

Charlie stood up from the fallen timber, lifted his

flouncy sleeves and patted Belle's tears with the linen, putting dirty stains on the white cloth.

'I have to find the book and give it back to Descartes,' he said.

'But why is the book so important? Why do you care about Descartes? You do not even know him.'

An eerie mist descended upon the forest. Charlie glimpsed at the canopy above, hoping to see a sign from Ted, or anything that would give Belle some answers. Nothing came. Nothing. Instead, the bitter winds whipped down the path and through the narrow forest corridor, stirring leaves at Charlie's ankles until his shoes and socks were covered.

'Please tell me,' Belle insisted. 'What is all this about, Charlie?'

Charlie tried to gather his thoughts. *What is this all about? Descartes' book has been stolen. Ted says I have to find it and give it back. A demon is somewhere here, in Descartes' mind, trying to control the Frenchman's thoughts — and it has the book. And a bird has stolen my Key.*

Charlie put the Key out of his mind. Even though he knew it was his ticket home. He had to focus on finding the book. That's what Ted wanted him to do. He felt like breaking down and curling into a ball, crying his heart out. But he couldn't do that either. It wouldn't achieve anything. Or would it? He shook his head, sucking in some more freezing air.

'A demon is here somewhere, Belle, with

Descartes' book. We have to find it,' said Charlie.

'But how do you know?' said Belle.

'Descartes told us.'

'He is a philosopher,' said Belle. 'They say strange things all the time.'

'Yeah, but Descartes was crying, because he thinks he's not in control of his own thoughts – and maybe a demon is?'

'But you have not answered my question. What is all this about?' Frustration crept into Belle's voice. 'I don't understand how any of this *affects you*?'

Charlie scanned the tree tops of the murky forest. The image of Ted with his dark rings and pasty skin entered his head. He went quiet for a moment. He had to tell her.

'This demon is not just hurting Descartes, it is hurting someone else — someone really special to me.'

'Who?'

'My grandfather, Ted,' whispered Charlie. 'He died recently.'

'How can a demon hurt a dead person?'

'Dead people aren't really dead,' replied Charlie. 'They have a soul – and they go to an Eternal World.'

'Descartes talks about the soul,' said Belle. 'He says it is made up of the same substance as the mind.'

'Yep,' said Charlie. 'The demon can move between the mind and the soul – and it did. It went to the Eternal World and zapped Ted of all of his energy, made him sick. And now it's zapping all of Ted's friends, making them sick as well.'

Silence fell upon Belle.

'I have to help my grandfather.' Charlie started shuffling along the remnants of what looked like a path. 'And I know the demon is here. I can feel it.'

'You are right Charlie, the demon *is* here somewhere,' she said eventually. 'I can feel it too.'

Belle kicked leaves and followed Charlie.

Just as the path disappeared completely, Charlie noticed that the trees became sparse and the canopy overheard began to clear. He spotted an unsettling moon rising. In front of him appeared an old headstone, covered in moss, tilted forward and looking ready to topple over. Behind it, he saw another. And another. And another.

'It's a graveyard!' said Charlie.

His words, although not particularly loud, echoed strangely across the cemetery. They came back to him, as if everyone who had ever been buried there had whispered *It's a graveyard... it's a graveyard... it's a graveyard...* back.

As Charlie's eyes skated over the vast burial ground, they came to a stop on a large dome-shaped headstone, bigger than the others, with a big white crucifix sticking out of the top.

'See that.' Charlie pointed. 'Come on!'

They zigzagged between the crooked tombstones,

which cast unnaturally long shadows that all seemed to be pointing to the crucifix.

Resting his hand at the base of the round memorial, Charlie felt the cold granite suddenly become warm under his fingertips. He quickly pulled his hand away. Slowly, he reached out his fingers and touched the granite again. The warmth radiated through him, and heated his heart, as though it was trying to comfort him.

'Touch this,' he said.

Belle touched the warm stone. She stared at Charlie, puzzled.

Charlie leaned over the tombstone and read the inscription out loud. 'Francine Descartes, five years old. Taken too early by Scarlet Fever. 7-9-1640.'

'It is Descartes' little girl.' Belle's eyes became glassy. She paused for a minute and eventually said, 'Her death was the greatest sorrow of his life.'

'Well… She's right here,' whispered Charlie. 'In the middle of Descartes' mind.'

Charlie examined the headstone closely. Tracing with his finger the inscription etched into the granite. He noticed that the *7* and *9* had been painted in gold, but the *1640* had been painted in silver.

'Poor Francine.' Belle plucked a lilac flower jutting out from a vase at the foot of the headstone. 'She was the star in his eyes.'

Without warning, Charlie jumped on the grave

and started to climb the dome of Francine's headstone.

'That is disrespectful,' snapped Belle.

'The demon is close.' Charlie balanced on top of the dome, using the headstone as a lookout tower. 'I can feel it watching us… But something tells me that Descartes is here too, trying to help us. The cabinet, the rusty sign, the pictures on the flap, he's trying to lead us somewhere.'

'Yes, but where?' Belle's eyes skimmed across the cemetery.

Charlie gripped the marble crucifix as he searched for a clue. 'This place is creepy.' As he spoke, the mist across the cemetery began to lift.

'Look!' he pointed.

'What is it?' Belle's head turned and she squinted.

'A church.' Charlie scrutinised the piercing steeple rising from the fog, stretching towards the stars as though it had escaped earth. 'Come on!'

Charlie leapt from the sacred shrine, toppling the vase packed with the lilacs and smashing it into a thousand pieces.

Making dents in the ice as they ran, the pair dashed towards the church. The steeple towered over them, now fully illuminated by a large blue moon, protruding against a backdrop of gloomy clouds.

13

THE CARTESIAN COORDINATES

As Charlie raced up the church's icy stone steps, he thought he saw a man in the shadows holding a melon. He remembered Descartes' dream about the ghosts and how he tried to find refuge in a church. He shook his head, blinked his eyelids and looked again. No one. If there was someone there, he had gone now. He rattled the ringed handles on the heavy iron doors.

'Locked,' he said.

'There must be a side entrance.' Belle disappeared into the fog down one side of the church.

In the moonlight, Charlie studied the double iron doors under a gothic arch, triple his height. Strange metal inlays decorated the doors, that looked like trees branching out from the sides. A strip of light filtered through a narrow gap in the middle. Charlie tried to line up his eye with the thin opening and peer in. He could see candles burning along one wall, but he couldn't make out much else.

Belle reappeared from the fog on the other side of the church.

'There is no way in,' she said.

As she made her announcement, she scooped up a dead sparrow lying on the bottom of the church steps, frozen solid.

'Wonderful,' she said.

Clutching the bird by its long-wedged tail, she inspected the grey-brown feathers around its throat. She stuffed the unfortunate creature into her coat, the foot snapping off as she pocketed it.

'What's that for?' asked Charlie.

'Dinner.'

She is always thinking about food, thought Charlie. His shoulders shivered, then he focused back on opening the doors.

'We need better light,' he said.

'I will get some.' Belle disappeared back into the cemetery, she weaved amongst the headstones.

From a grave nearby, Charlie saw her snatch a candle from a stony-faced angel. Delighted with her find, she bounced up the steps and lay the candle carefully on the snow. She pulled a strange piece of metal, shaped like knuckle dusters, from one of her inside coat pockets. From another pocket, she extracted a small cloth and her knife. Placing the cloth carefully under the knuckle dusters, she whacked the metal violently with her knife.

Clang. Clang. Clang.

Booming clanks rang across the graveyard.

Charlie's whole body shuddered with every whack. He threw his fingers to his ears and glared at Belle. But then sparks started to fly from the metal. The cloth ignited. Belle lifted the candle and lit the wick from the cloth. She put her boot on the smouldering material, stamping out the flames, and handed the candle to Charlie.

'Thanks!' Charlie grinned and wondered what else she had in those pockets. Thinking about it a bit more, he decided he didn't want to know. He hovered the flame close to the doors.

Under the flickering candlelight, he examined some writing carved between the iron inlays, not in his language.

'That writing.' He pointed. 'Can you see it?'

Belle leaned forward. 'It is Latin.'

'Can you read Latin?' asked Charlie.

'Of course.'

Charlie didn't know why he was surprised, but he was. In his mind, Belle looked like a girl who probably wouldn't even attend school. How could she possibly know how to read Latin? But he was pleased she could.

'Descartes teaches me it,' she added, as if she was reading Charlie's thoughts.

She squinted as Charlie held the candle against the doors. 'Entry lies at the *Cartesian Coordinates*.'

'What does that mean?' said Charlie.

'Cartesian Coordinates,' Belle's eye's glazed over.

Charlie could see that her mind was pondering the words.

'Cartesian Coordinates,' he repeated, trying to prompt her to say something.

'Yes, they are a system that Descartes has dreamt up.'

'A system? What is it?'

'It is funny. He uses it to draw squares and circles and curves from all these strange equations he likes to work on. He also uses it to locate things. He does it all on just two simple lines.'

She moved to the church's railing and snapped off a wooden picket that dangled from the bannister like a broken toothpick. She scraped the picket along the snow.

'What are you doing?' asked Charlie.

'I am showing you Descartes' Cartesian Coordinates — how they work.'

She pointed with the picket to the horizontal line

she had just drawn. 'He calls this line the X axis.'

Charlie shivered. He remembered sitting in the exam room.

Next, she drew a vertical line that crossed the horizontal line in the middle. 'This line is called the Y axis.'

'Yep,' said Charlie. 'I've heard about the X and the Y axis before.'

Belle smiled at Charlie, but she did look somewhat surprised.

With the stick, she wrote numbers along the X line: *-5, -4, -3, -2, -1,* and *0* where the lines crossed, and then *1, 2, 3, 4, 5.* On the vertical Y line, she wrote *-5, -4, -3, -2, -1* below the X line, and *1, 2, 3, 4, 5* above it.

'Descartes says that you can know the location of anything just by using two numbers.' Belle seemed to thrive on Charlie's attention. 'So, let us choose numbers 2 and 3.'

She scraped the rod across the ice. 'See, if you go two spaces along the X line and three spaces up the Y line your location is here.' She tapped the stone like a teacher taps a blackboard. 'So, the *coordinates* are two and three — and that is your location.'

'I get that,' said Charlie. His mind flashed back to the exam paper. He remembered Question Eight and staring blankly at the numbers 22 and 16. He recalled how he had to plot one more point on the grid to finish the line graph, but he couldn't do it. His mind had frozen in the exam, but for some reason his mind wasn't freezing now.

'It's like a graph,' he said suddenly.

'Yes.' Belle grinned. She seemed impressed that Charlie knew what a graph was. 'It is a graph — Descartes invented the graph,' she added.

So he is the culprit, thought Charlie, *for all that dumb homework I have to do.*

He read the inscription again.

'*Entry lies at the Cartesian Coordinates* — but what are the coordinates? And how do we get into the church?' He heaved a sigh.

Belle shrugged her shoulders, unhelpfully.

Under the soft candle flame, Charlie knelt down until he was at eye-level with the metal ringed handles. He had seen these ancient lock mechanisms before — at the museum with Ted. He jingled the handles. He remembered the pin on his jacket that had been clipped to the watch. In an instant, he unfastened it. With his fingers he smoothed it into a flat piece of wire.

'What are you doing?' asked Belle.

'I'm going to try and pick it,' said Charlie.

'You can do that?'

'Most of the time.' Charlie jangled the wire in the hole. 'That is weird.'

'What is?' asked Belle.

'There should be a rod,' said Charlie. 'It should be attached to the handle and then pass through a hole in the door. It connects to a pivot on the back of a metal plate on the other side. When the handle is turned, a latch lifts from the plate, and the door opens.'

'And the rod is not there?' asked Belle.

'No,' said Charlie surprised. 'It's like these handles have been stuck on the doors for show.'

Charlie shoved the wire into the pocket of his balloon pants. His eyes became drawn to the stone step under his feet. He expected to see a worn entrance, but there was no wear and tear. *This is not the entrance at all*, he thought. He remembered a book that Ted owned about the ancient pyramids of Giza. Archaeologists had discovered some secret chambers hidden in the depths of the pyramids that were only accessible by underground tunnels. He recalled that the entry points of the tunnels were quite a distance from the pyramids themselves. Turning his back on the doors, his eyes combed the graveyard.

'Cartesian Coordinates,' Charlie whispered. 'Something tells me the entry to the church is out there somewhere.'

Belle turned her body with Charlie's, her eyes also scanning the cemetery. After a long moment she said, 'Look at that.'

'Look at what?' Charlie asked.

'The paths.' Belle pointed to the path in front of her and drew a vertical line in the air with her finger. 'That path looks like the Y axis.' Her finger changed direction and she air-crossed the line she had just drawn. 'And that path is the X axis.'

'You're right, Belle.' Charlie moved closer to the edge of the step. 'The paths in the graveyard are the X and Y lines.'

Charlie noticed the white marble crucifix on top of Francine's headstone. His eyes expanded. 'And Francine's headstone is right where the X and Y lines cross.' He scrutinised the gravestones, neatly in rows and perfectly positioned with the vertical and horizontal paths between them.

'I don't know why I didn't notice this before,' gasped Charlie. 'This graveyard is one massive grid.'

Charlie glared at Belle and sighed. 'But what are the coordinates? What are the two numbers?'

Belle shrugged.

'Wait…' said Charlie. 'There are numbers on Francine's grave.'

'Numbers,' said Belle. 'The only numbers are from the date she died.'

'Yes, but they're still numbers,' said Charlie. 'There was a seven and a nine painted in gold. The other numbers were in silver. Could they be the coordinates?'

'Maybe,' said Belle.

She itched her head. 'Anything gilded in gold is important.'

'It must be the two numbers.' Charlie smiled. 'Descartes has put the coordinates in gold for us — on Francine's headstone. He's helping us again. He's helping us get into the church. Quick!' Charlie pounded down the steps of the church and raced back towards Francine's headstone.

Arooooooooooooooooooooo!

Half way down the path a long strange sound came from the edge of the graveyard. Charlie stopped in his tracks. His ears pricked up. The noise sounded like a foghorn on a barge, but it became louder, and went on and on, at different pitches. He felt the vines rustling at his feet, as if they too were scared of the terrifying sound.

14

THE OBELISK

'What was that?' Charlie froze.

'I do not know.' Belle rammed into his back.

Charlie set off again, quickening his pace towards Francine's grave.

When they reached the grave, they both stared at the numbers, *7* and *9*.

'Right,' said Charlie. 'Francine's grave must be the centre point, zero. Which means we go seven graves down that way.' He pointed to his right.

Aroooooooooooooooooooo!

The barge sound came again, only this time more spine-chilling.

'What *is* that noise?' snapped Charlie.

'Hurry,' said Belle.

Stepping up the pace, Charlie counted, 'One, two, three…' The vines swished around his ankles. Belle counted headstones with him, partially concealed by creepers as they passed. They both came to a stop in front of grave number seven.

'OK, now we move nine up this way.' Charlie waved his hand.

'Are you sure?' said Belle.

'It's the coordinate.' Charlie counted once more, 'One, two, three…'

The wails came again. Louder and louder. The harrowing howls were close now. A sudden wind blustered around them, but not strong enough to muffle out the disturbing sound.

Charlie stared in the direction of the terrifying noise and continued counting. 'Seven, eight, nine.'

With narrowed eyes he spotted a jet-black figure, zooming across the night sky. A thunderous flapping sound rumbled down his eardrums. Was it the raven? He squinted in the direction of the creature. It was too dark to make out the blurred figure.

Suddenly, a ghostly looking animal with a greyish body and a white face emerged from the shadows on the edge of the woods.

'Is that a dog?' asked Charlie.

Belle jolted her head in the direction of the creature. 'Oh no!'

'What *is it*?'

'A wolf.'

Charlie watched the creature as it dipped its head and straightened its two front legs, as though it was doing stretches. Then a second wolf appeared behind it.

'Two wolves,' Belle whispered.

Another came from the shadows. And another. And another. With his eyes popping from his skull, Charlie made out hundreds of them.

Throat clamming up now, Charlie changed his focus away from the wolfpack and towards grave number nine. This headstone didn't look like the others. A giant obelisk as high as a house, sat smothered in ivy. Charlie started to climb it, using a series of narrow ledges spaced out evenly up the monument as footing. When he reached the top, he whipped his hands at the creepers, trying to find an inscription. Nothing.

But then, amongst the leaves, he spied a strange image of what looked like a solar system. The sun was in the centre with planet rings circling it, all carved delicately into the stone. Using the ledges, he moved to the opposite side of the monument. Ripping away more vines, he found a large spoked wheel sticking out of the stone.

'What is it?' shouted Belle.

'It's a wheel of some sort,' said Charlie.

'Can you turn it?' Belle began to climb the obelisk

up the ledges, one eye on her footing, the other on the wolves.

'I'll try.' Charlie placed his fingers on the icy spokes and tried to shift the wheel. Heaving with all his might, the veins in his neck bulged. The wheel didn't budge. He shifted his leg position, changed grip, this time using his back and shoulder muscles. The wheel started to turn.

Wruuuuuuk.

'Something's happening,' said Charlie. 'But I'm not sure what.'

Charlie gripped the wheel even tighter. He wrestled the spokes with grinding force.

Wruuuuuuk. Wruuuuuuk.

'The sun picture.' Belle pointed. 'It is opening.'

'What do you mean it's opening?' said Charlie, from the opposite side of the obelisk. 'I can't see it.'

'It is like there is a hole in the sun, and it is getting bigger when you turn the wheel,' said Belle. 'Turn it again.'

'The passageway into the church,' said Charlie. 'Can you fit into it?'

'Not yet,' said Belle. 'Keep turning.'

Charlie put his back into it. He grinded the wheel as hard as he could.

'Look!' shrieked Belle. She pointed to the sky. 'The raven!'

A flash of black caught Charlie's eye. To his

horror, he watched the bird dart past the silhouette of the moon, take a sharp turn and nose-dive, straight in the direction of the wolfpack leader. From Charlie's vantage point, he could see the bird ram its razor-sharp beak right between the wolf's ears. The bird did a U-turn and rocketed skyward, disappearing into the haze.

The front wolf snapped back its legs, bared its fangs and howled. The other hounds crouched and cocked their tails. Then, with wild threatening eyes, the whole pack stampeded. Long powerful legs pounded the crisp white snow into huge plume balls, heading straight for Charlie and Belle.

Grrrrrrrrrrrrrrrrrrrrrr.

The earth rumbled.

'Hurry!' screamed Belle. 'They are charging us!'

Charlie twisted the wheel.

Belle shifted her boots to a higher ledge, so she could peer down the opening.

'What's in there?' Charlie heaved at the wheel again.

'It is pitch black,' came the reply. 'I cannot see.'

'Can you get in?' The hounds' stampede rumbled the graveyard.

'I will try!'

Paws hammering the ice drilled down Charlie's eardrums.

Grrrrrrrrrrrrrrrrrrrrrr.

Another heave. Charlie hoped the hole was big enough for Belle.

'Can you get in now?' he yelled again.

Arms first, Belle's head disappeared, her body horizontal and her legs kicking.

'I am stuck!' she shouted.

Wruuuuuuk.

Charlie grinded the wheel, trying to make the hole even larger. 'What about now?'

'No!' Belle cried.

'The wheel is stuck,' gasped Charlie. 'I can't turn it anymore.'

Grrrrrrrrrrrrrrrrrrrrrr.

The wolves charged the obelisk and circled the base like racing cars. Knife-sharp fangs snapped at Charlie and Belle's heels. Rotten flesh and saliva dribbled from the tongues of the canine beasts, hissing and snarling like poltergeists, the dogs ready to slice their limbs into strips.

'Help!' screeched Belle.

'I'm coming!' Charlie's hands left the wheel. Balancing on his toes, he scaled the narrow ledge to the opposite side of the obelisk. At the sun-hole, Belle's lower body dangled from the opening, her feet swinging. Her upper body was inside the monument, with her heavy brown coat squished in firmly around her waist.

'I'm going to push you.' Seeing how tightly Belle

was packed into that hole, even Charlie thought his plan was dubious.

'Be careful,' she said.

'I'm grabbing your legs.'

Charlie gripped Belle's ankles. He felt her calf muscles tense. She kicked her shoes and her midriff wriggled.

'Can you move?' screamed Charlie.

'No!' she barked.

In that second, a wolf leapt into the air. The wild eyes of the beast scowled at Charlie. He tried to slap the monster down. But its needle-like claws punctured holes into Belle's ankle. Blood spurted from the puncture wounds.

'*Owwww!*' Belle's gut-wrenching wails echoed across the graveyard like a wounded hyena.

15

THE CHURCH PEWS

The wolf leapt again. This time drilling its fangs into Belle's coat, but staying there. The creature swung wildly from the hem.

'It's after the sparrow!' shouted Charlie. 'It can smell it!'

'I cannot reach it!' snarled Belle.

One of Charlie's hands released Belle's ankle. He lunged forward, threw his hand in her coat pocket, scrounging around for the sparrow's tail. He whipped it out and tossed the feathery stiff right past the wolf's slimy nostrils. Whiffing the bird's scent, the hound unlocked its incisors from the coat, as the dead sparrow bounced across the ice.

Pouncing onto the lifeless bird, the wolf devoured

the chunk of meat in a nanosecond. Blood oozed out from the feathers and seeped into the snow.

Changing his footing, Charlie gripped Belle's legs again.

'I'm going to push you,' he shouted. 'Put your hands out!'

'They are out!' she cried.

The weight of Belle, or her coat, caused Charlie's neck veins to bulge. With all his might, he shoved her legs into the hole. He held them for as long as he could, worried that she would drop hard, head first.

Thud!

Charlie heard her land heavily.

'Are you alright?' he yelled.

'I am alive,' came the muffled response.

Lifting his own body weight, he scrambled head-first into the sun hole. From inside the obelisk, the sound of snapping jaws softened. Charlie stretched out his arms into a dive position and shut tight his eyes. He wriggled his waist forward, further into the hole, until he could feel his body about to fall.

'I'm coming down!'

Thud!

He landed next to Belle.

'That was close,' he whispered.

'They ate my dinner,' Belle sighed.

Charlie heard the disappointment in her voice. 'You'll find another bird.'

Belle sat upright. Under a thin ray of moonlight trickling through the sun hole above, she examined her bleeding ankle.

'We need to bandage that,' said Charlie.

Unbuttoning his purple jacket, he tossed it on the dirt. He ripped off a whole sleeve from his flouncy white shirt underneath. 'We'll use this.'

Belle watched Charlie carefully wrap her ankle.

'Thank you,' she said.

Once the wound had been wrapped, Charlie helped lift Belle to her feet. She stumbled at first, but could walk on it.

'You were right.' Belle pointed to a narrow passageway that led away from the empty tomb. 'It is indeed a tunnel.'

'We need another candle,' said Charlie.

Belle pulled the old candle from her pocket, together with her knuckle dusters. This time she whacked the strange bit of equipment against the stone wall. Sparks flew everywhere. Before Charlie knew it, the candle was burning in front of Belle's piercing green eyes.

'This way,' she said.

Admiring her resourcefulness, Charlie crept along the narrow passageway behind her, inhaling the sweet scent of beeswax. At the end of the tunnel, they climbed three sets of rickety stairs. On the top step, Belle pushed on the handle of an arched door.

They entered a small room to the side of the church.

'The vestibule,' announced Belle.

Charlie shuffled past a big timber cross attached to the wall, and a dark painting of the Virgin Mary cradling baby Jesus, both with halos circling their heads. He followed Belle down a side aisle into the main body of the church.

'There's a girl in here.' Charlie pointed.

In front of the altar, a small girl in a pink dress sat on a pew, her face covered by a prayer book. Mumbles came from the child, like she was reciting a prayer.

'Shoosh.' Belle lifted her finger to her lips. 'She is praying. We do not disturb her. We will go to the rear.'

Charlie tottered behind Belle to the back of the church, which seemed much bigger inside that it ever did outside.

The leadlight windows flashed patterns of blue, yellow and red across their faces as they sat on the last pew at the back. In silence, they stared at the altar with its white pasty candles flickering a strange orange glow.

'Why are we in a church?' whispered Charlie. 'Why did Descartes lead us here?'

'I do not know,' said Belle.

'Weird,' said Charlie.

They sat for some time in silence.

'Do you believe in God?' asked Charlie abruptly.

'Yes,' replied Belle. 'I am sure he exists.'

'How can you be so sure?'

'Because Descartes is certain God exists,' replied Belle.

Charlie didn't know much about God, but since Ted's death, he knew plenty about the Eternal World. So, who knows? Maybe there was a God there as well. Although he sure hadn't seen him.

'But how can Descartes be sure?' asked Charlie.

Belle's eyes became wider, as though she was pleased with Charlie's question.

'Have you ever had an idea Charlie, that maybe a perfect God exists?'

'I suppose I have had an idea,' he said. 'But it's just an idea — it's not proof.'

'But Charlie, think for a moment, where did that idea come from?'

'I don't know,' said Charlie. 'Maybe I just thought it up.'

'No, Charlie. Descartes says you do not just think ideas up about God.'

'Why not?'

'Descartes says that the idea of God is too clear in his mind. He says he thinks he knows more about God than he does about any other creature on earth, including himself.'

'Interesting,' said Charlie.

'And so, if Descartes idea of a perfect God is so clear,' Belle grinned. 'Where must the idea have come from? Could it come from a person so imperfect such as Descartes?'

Belle's eyes locked with Charlie's.

'From God,' said Charlie. 'The idea of God must have come from God.'

Belle smiled warmly at Charlie.

'From a perfect God.' She nodded. 'And if Descartes' idea came from a perfect God — what does that prove?'

'That God exists,' whispered Charlie.

In that split second, Charlie thought he saw a set of black wings glide across the church's rafters behind the altar. He squinted, staring at the roof, but he couldn't see the bird.

'Come on,' he whispered.

Charlie leapt from his pew and scuffled quickly down the centre aisle of the nave. Belle tailed him. Passing the little girl sitting near the front of the altar, Charlie heard her recite a prayer from her prayer book. *That's strange*, thought Charlie, *she's saying the same thing over and over again.*

'What language is that?' he whispered.

'Latin,' came Belle's reply.

Careful not to disturb the young girl praying, Belle pointed to an open door leading into the sacristy behind the altar. 'I think it flew in there.'

Charlie skipped behind the altar and tiptoed towards the open door. He entered a long rectangular room, lined either side by a row of narrow arched windows, covered in leadlight with religious pictures. High-backed chairs were positioned directly under each window.

As Charlie walked along the room, a silhouette of man sitting in a chair, right down the far end of the room, came into vision. He squinted in the darkness.

'Hello,' he said.

No answer.

He moved in for a closer look, and thought he recognised the man.

'Descartes,' he said. 'Is that you?'

Hearing Charlie say the name, Belle dashed towards the man. But stopped suddenly when she saw Descartes strapped to a chair with heavy chains wrapped around his neck, wrists and ankles.

'Descartes,' shrieked Belle. 'What happened?'

He groaned.

Descartes tried to lift his head to acknowledge Belle, but he didn't have any strength. Strange bits of tubing protruded from his head and joined a large machine sitting alongside of him. The Frenchman sat motionless, with his deep sunken eyes. Charlie watched his chest rise and fall.

'Tell us what happened,' Belle reached for his

flaccid hand. But just as she touched him, her hand moved right through Descartes' body as though the person was a ghost. She couldn't feel him. He wasn't there.

She squealed.

Belle and Charlie jumped back from the chair and stared at the apparition.

'Don't be frightened, I am here in mind,' said Descartes. 'Not body.'

Charlie and Belle took another step further away.

'It is alright,' Descartes insisted. He motioned his hand to them to move closer. The Frenchman lifted his heavy eyelids as he tried to focus.

'What happened to you?' said Belle again. 'Why are you chained?'

'It is the evil demon,' whispered Descartes. His voice weak and raspy. 'It is too late.'

'What do you mean?' asked Charlie. 'It's too late.'

'It came here.' Descartes' eyes darted around the church. 'It came here to me, and stood there, laughing and laughing.'

'What about the book?' said Charlie. 'Did you see the book?'

'Oh yes,' replied Descartes. 'The demon had it in his claws. He tossed it in the air and said he was in control of my thoughts now. Then my manuscript exploded into flames, right in front of my very eyes.'

'Exploded,' repeated Charlie.

'Yes.' Descartes sighed. 'The book has gone.'

Charlie felt a dagger plunge into the depths of his chest. He moved away from Descartes and toward the arched window, squinting through the dirty glass. *How can the book be gone?* He thought. *What do I do now?*

'You must leave here,' said Descartes as though he was reading Charlie's mind.

'It is too dangerous to stay,' Descartes gasped. 'The demon has won — my mind is his. Leave now before it controls your mind as well.'

'But what about you?' asked Belle. 'You can't stay here.'

'My thoughts are useless now. They are not mine. What is a person without thoughts? Nothing but a puppet on a string. Go, go now, for your own good.'

An unnatural icy wind stirred around the pockets of the church. Prayer cards fluttered from a table and scattered across the tiles. The wind started to push Charlie and Belle away from the apparition. It blasted them out of the rectangular room into the main body of the church. The little girl in the pink dress had vanished. Then the church's front doors flung open and swept them out of the cathedral and back onto the front steps.

16

THE COLOUR OF THE SPIRE

Outside the church, Charlie slumped onto the icy-cold steps, holding his head in his hands. Belle slumped next to him.

Charlie didn't know what to do next. How could he do what Ted had asked when the book had been burnt to a crisp? What did all this mean for Ted? What did it mean for all of those faces in the sky?

I tried to save you, Ted, Charlie thought. *But I couldn't. I'm sorry. I am so sorry.*

Tears pooled in Charlie's eyes. He heaved a massive sigh and gazed up to the night sky, seeking Ted's forgiveness. Nothing came.

'I am such a loser,' he whispered.

'You tried.' Belle threw an arm around his shoulders.

'Yeah, but it wasn't good enough,' said Charlie. 'Nothing I do is ever good enough.'

'Well…' whispered Belle. 'Nothing I do is ever good enough either.'

Charlie turned his head. 'How do you mean?'

'Look at me,' Belle sniffed. 'All I do is search for food. It is my job. If I do not do this my family goes hungry.'

'You have to feed your whole family?' said Charlie, surprised.

'Yes,' nodded Belle. 'My whole family.'

'But what about your parents?' asked Charlie. 'Why don't they get food?'

'They would if they were able.' Belle sighed. 'When I was small, our family had plenty of food. We lived at the castle. My father was a stone mason at Tre Kronor, the best that has ever been. He was renowned across the country for his lion heads. But one day all that changed.'

'What happened?' asked Charlie.

'He was working under the footbridge, carving a lion's head onto the pylon. Workers were on top of the bridge finishing the arch. A fight broke out between two of the men. They fought like cats and dogs. One of them toppled the other over and he slipped against the wall, pushing a stone block over the edge. The block landed on my father's arm and crushed it. Now his arm is a stump and he has not seen work since.' Belle sighed.

'Gee, that's pretty bad,' said Charlie.

'My father sits at home, stares blankly out the window, and carves miniature lions in timber with his good arm. Mother takes them to the market and she tries to sell them, but people in the village are poor, and there is little demand for miniatures.'

'That's awful.' Charlie shook his head.

'So now I have to find food for my family,' Belle snivelled. 'And the food is never enough. Descartes helps me sneak in and out of the castle. He knows I steal food, but he turns a blind eye.'

'How many brothers and sisters do you have?' asked Charlie.

'Eight.'

'Eight?' repeated Charlie.

Belle picked up a rock and tossed it down the steps.

Charlie started to feel guilty.

Poor Belle, he thought. *She's just a girl trying to feed her whole family and I was thinking she's nothing but a light-fingered thief. I've watched her steal things with my own eyes. But what do I know about her? What do I really know about anything? Nothing is ever what it seems.*

Beyond the graveyard, Charlie spied Tre Kronor castle in the distance. He watched the moonlight dance across the tower's spire that almost touched the stars. Standing up from the steps, Charlie studied the colours of the spire, which had changed from earlier in the evening.

'Tell me, Belle.' He pointed to the watchtower. 'What colour is that spire?'

Belle rose to her feet, focussed her eyes in the direction of the spire. She examined the colour carefully.

'It is kind of a dark blue-grey.'

'Yeah, but did you see it earlier tonight? What colour was it then?'

Belle thought about it for a second. 'I remember the sun on the horizon, the sky was a dusky pink… Yes… The spire was pink.'

'And if the sun was out at say midday, what colour would it be then?'

Belle stared at Charlie as if she was wondering where all these weird questions were going.

'It would be golden,' she said. 'Like gold itself.'

'Yes, golden.' Charlie nodded. 'So what colour is the spire?'

'Do you mean its real colour?' she whispered. 'I do not know.'

'Exactly,' said Charlie. 'What did Descartes say again about our senses?'

'Our senses deceive us,' sighed Belle. 'They don't speak the truth. We can never rely on them. Our mind is far more reliable.'

'Precisely,' said Charlie.

'But how does all this help us?'

'C'mon,' said Charlie. He motioned for Belle to go back into the church with him.

'Why are we going back in there?'

'We are in Descartes' mind. We have just seen a ghost of him sitting in a chair with chains. How do we know it was Descartes? How do we know what he said is true? How do we know the book has exploded into flames? How do we know anything? We can't trust our eyes. We can't trust our ears. We can't trust anything. This is what Descartes has been saying to us all along. We can't trust anything at all. We can only trust our minds.'

Charlie charged through the church's iron doors, and sprinted down the central aisle of the nave and into the sacristy. His footsteps echoed across the tiles and rattled the candlesticks jutting out of the walls. Belle ripped along behind. Darting past the altar towards the long rectangular room, Charlie heard the chains rattle. He stopped abruptly and froze.

'Hup!' Belle gasped.

In the shadows, a thin black figure of a man rose from the chair. The body-shape was not Descartes. It was someone else. Or something else.

With abnormally long fingernails, the creature clawed at the chains, and then slashed the tubes. It loomed a long neck and turned its head in the direction of Charlie. Two yellow eyes flashed like lasers.

Smash.

In a blink of eye, the figure escaped out the window.

Charlie chased after it. His leather heels skated across the broken glass. He dashed towards the arch and peered through the splinters protruding from the frame. He couldn't see the creature but watched a raven glide behind the spire, cross the sky and nestle in the three golden crowns of Tre Kronor's central tower.

'I'm going to the watchtower,' whispered Charlie. 'Nothing here is right – nothing is what it seems.'

'I am coming with you,' said Belle.

17

THE RODENTS

Behind a low-rise hedge, Charlie and Belle watched a guard pace up and down in front of the watchtower's gated entrance. Marching like he was stamping out hot coals, the soldier cupped his hands and blew into his thick gloves, trying desperately to escape the cold.

'How are we going to get past him?' said Belle. 'And the gate is padlocked.'

Charlie squinted at the lock. 'It's an apple padlock.'

'How do you know that?' said Belle.

'I've seen them before,' said Charlie. 'They were common in Europe about this time.'

'Can you open it?' asked Belle.

'I can try.' Charlie tapped the wire in his balloon pants. 'But we need to distract the guard.'

'Yes,' said Belle. 'We need a big distraction.'

Both pairs of eyes scanned the central courtyard and the white buildings surrounding it. Charlie could see hundreds of ravens, nested on the gables and the chimneys scattered across the blue copper roofs. A handful of the birds sat on a low stone wall, opposite the tower's gate, as though they were waiting for something to happen.

Charlie looked for the jet-black raven. He eyed the largest bird of them all, nestled in the three crowns above the tower's spire. Even from where Charlie stood, he could see the creature's yellow eyes, glowing and unnatural. Nothing was normal about that bird.

'There are so many,' said Belle. 'I have never seen so many birds here before.'

'Yeah,' said Charlie. 'But I only need one.'

He frowned at the giant bird nesting in-between the tips of the crowns.

'Do ravens eat bread?' he said suddenly.

'They prefer mice,' said Belle, sounding like a raven expert.

A smile crossed Belle's face like she was about to do something illegal. Her sparkling green irises skimmed the cobblestones, looking for rodents.

'It will not take us long to catch a dozen or so,'

she said.

'Mice,' cut in Charlie. 'You can't be serious… You want to catch mice?'

Charlie glared at Belle's smirking grin and the twinkle in her eye. She was deadly serious. How were they going to catch mice? Filthy little creatures, ridden with disease. Snaring mice just wasn't Charlie's thing. He couldn't think of anything more disgusting. Maybe he could. Catching rats.

Belle whisked off her beanie. 'We will put them into this.'

Charlie stared at the beanie, dotted with holes — like that was a good plan.

In seconds, Belle zipped into the courtyard's darkest corner. She pulled cheese from her pockets and held it steady in her hand. From where Charlie stood, he could see the ground near Belle move. Scratching, scrambling and squeaking. Hundreds of them! They scampered down walls, slipped through tiny cracks in the bricks and some even fell from the beams supporting the turrets.

Hair rose on the back of Charlie's neck as he watched the invasion. Where had they all come from? Jumping over each other, going wild, all over the slightest whiff of cheese. Sickly looking things they were too — blood on their noses, scabs on their ears. Charlie threw his hand to his mouth and gagged.

'Come.' Belle waved at Charlie. 'Hold my hat — I

will trap them!'

Smack.

A mouse landed on Charlie's head and rustled through his hair. He slapped his head wildly until it hurt. The rodent darted into his ruffles behind his neck. Charlie felt tiny hooks scratch his upper back. He sucked in a scream.

The creature slipped down his spine, like a furry chunk of ice. He bit his lip. Frantically, he rummaged his hands up his shirt. Tiny claws ripped across his skin. Seconds later, the rodent dropped on the stone. Charlie felt like squashing it with his heel, but he thought better of it. The rodent escaped into the darkness.

Racing around madly, Belle seized as many mice as she could. Not scared one bit, she looked more like she was enjoying herself.

Charlie studied her technique. Step on their tails first, so the pesky little critters couldn't move. With her thumb and forefinger, she hoisted them up until at eye level, grinning and watching their legs kick. After a second watching them squirm, she tossed them into her beanie. Charlie had to quickly seal the beanie each time, so the others didn't escape. Long tails and twisted legs dangled from the opening.

'How many have we got?' asked Belle.

'About ten,' replied Charlie. He had no idea how many, he just didn't want to hold the stupid hat anymore.

'That will be enough,' said Belle, sounding like an expert again.

Charlie followed Belle from the shadows back to the low-rise hedge. As he crept along, the beanie wriggled in his palms and squeaks of panic came through the wool. Charlie tried to smother the noise with his hands, but nothing stopped the terrified mousy shrieks.

Crouching down, a serious look spread over Belle's face.

'When I say *now*,' she whispered. 'We run through the tower's gate.'

Charlie nodded.

Belle snatched the beanie from Charlie fingers. Her arm flew backwards, and she tossed the hat in the air. It flew over the courtyard like a basketball. Landing behind the guard's boot, the mice scrambled out of the beanie in every possible direction.

Charlie watched the little critters sprinting for their pocket-sized lives. One of them dashed towards the guard, straight up his trouser leg. The soldier whacked his palms hard against his thighs trying to snuff out the rodent.

Within seconds, hundreds of wings launched into flight and thundered across the skies. The ravens circled overhead, high above the castle's copper roofs, selecting their victims. They swooped on the helpless creatures. Squawks and squeals echoed beyond the courtyard as dark-grey beaks and ice-picked claws began dissecting their prey.

The raven nestling in the three golden crowns didn't move. It watched though. Beady yellow eyes glued to the chaos. After a minute of observing the massacre, the creature reared on its prickly legs and spanned its wings, as though signalling to Charlie it was about to challenge him. The bird's wings started thrashing. It propelled from its perch into the dark night, flying higher and higher — much higher than the other birds.

Suddenly, it changed direction and plunged at Charlie. Piercing squawks rang around the courtyard like a deafening siren. Charlie's hands flew to his head as he ducked. In that moment, Charlie spotted the book tucked underneath the bird's crusty claws. He lunged at it. Missed. The raven screeched. Then the bird retreated skyward and settled back into the golden crowns.

Enraged by the madness, the guard sprinted from his post. He dashed into the middle of the yard. His musket dropped from his back, he whipped gunpowder down the barrels. Pointing the weapon at the swarm of black birds overhead, he opened fire.

Poomb.

More gunpowder shoved down the barrels.

Poomb.

More gunpowder.

Poomb.

Again, and again, the guard fired the gun at the birds.

Charlie pressed his hands against his ears. His shoulders shuddered at each set of explosions.

'Now!' yelled Belle.

18

THE WATCHTOWER

Charlie jumped the low-rise hedge and dashed across the courtyard. Belle sprinted after him, her eyes fixed on the guard shooting at the birds, who had his back to them. Jet black ravens flapped over their heads and zoomed in every direction.

Charging towards the gate at the base of the watchtower, Charlie pulled out his wire as he ran. He snatched the apple-shaped padlock in his hand and quickly pushed the wire in at the front, right where the key normally goes. He twisted the wire. The spring-loaded bolt shifted sideways and the hinged shackle sprung open. The lock dropped from the gate.

'Brilliant!' Belle grinned.

Shoving the gate open, Charlie raced into the watchtower and jumped on a rickety ladder. His leather shoes pummelled the rungs. He climbed the ladder towards a hole in the roof. After reaching the first floor, he scrambled off the ladder, stepped a couple of paces sideways, and climbed onto a second ladder that led to another hole in the roof. He pummelled the rungs again. Belle scrambled behind him, panting like a dog in her heavy coat. Second floor. New Ladder. Third floor. New ladder. Fourth Floor. New ladder. Fifth Floor.

'Aarrgh!' Charlie's foot smashed through a rotten rung on the sixth ladder.

Huge timber splinters pinned his left foot either side. He tugged hard, stuck in the shards, and watched his skin peel off his ankle like old paint. Sucking up the pain, and with teeth gritted, he kept climbing. Higher and higher, hunting down the bird.

When Charlie reached the seventh level, he climbed off the ladder, hunched over and gripped his knees. His chest wheezed.

He glared at the ladder opposite. 'How many levels are there in this tower?'

'Nine,' replied Belle, trying to catch her own breath. 'Nine — until we reach the viewing platform.'

Sucking in a gallon of air, Charlie put his pointers on the bottom rung of the eighth ladder. With a huge amount of effort, he painfully lifted his limbs, every bone in his body aching.

Finally, Charlie reached the ninth floor — the viewing platform. In a flurry of snow, he skated towards a battered timber railing that circled the platform. The barrier was so wobbly, it wouldn't meet safety standards anywhere.

From this vantage point, Charlie could see everything. Everything. The guard in the courtyard below was still shooting at the ravens with his giant musket. Charlie's eyes followed the horizontal X path across the graveyard until it crossed the vertical Y path with Francine's crucifix grave in the middle. He even counted the coordinates, seven across, nine up, and spotted the grave with the sun-hole that had led them to the church.

Whoosh. Whoosh.

Above his head, he heard beating wings.

Aaaaaaark.

An ear-splitting squawk rang out from the golden crowns above. The siren reverberated over the fortress's rooftops and beyond into the deepest depths of the woodlands. Charlie gripped a timber post supporting the spire, shut his eyelids and jumped up, onto the weather-beaten railing. To his surprise he didn't crash through it.

Belle finally reached the platform. 'What are you going to do?'

'I'm climbing the spire,' said Charlie.

'You cannot go up there.' Belle's eyes scanned the rickety structure as her hair jumbled in a gust. 'You will be blown off.'

'I have to,' said Charlie. A frozen wind blasted through his body. 'That bird has the book.'

Charlie gripped the timber under-beam, just below the spire. He lifted his body up, as if doing a chin up. When his waist was level to the edge of the spire's copper plates, he mounted the pointed roof. With the tips of his fingers pressing on the plates, he slowly clambered up the spire. Snow fluttered into his eyes and icicles started to form on his earlobes. His body shivered. He dared not to look down, knowing one slip would be certain death.

Half way up, he glanced at the metal rod protruding from the tip of the spire. The three golden crowns on the end of the rod shimmered like a monster's three pronged claws. Charlie's heartbeat went into overdrive.

No choice. He had to keep climbing. With his knees rattling, Charlie inched his way carefully up the icy plates, shredding his fingertips on the sharp copper edges. When he reached the metal rod, he grabbed it with a clenched fist and hung on to it for dear life.

Charlie's eyes rolled upwards. Nestled in the three crowns, the raven flashed its yellow eyes directly at Charlie. But something about those yellow eyes didn't sit well with him. Glowing and luminous, they didn't look natural.

The creature rose from the crowns and started to beat its mammoth wings. Speckles of dust drifted from the black feathers and became illuminated like tiny fireflies under the starlight.

Charlie stared at the paranormal yellow eyes again. His own eyes widened.

'You're not a bird!' he shouted.

In a flash, a crack of thunder exploded across the clouds. Shrieks from the raven rang down the spire and over the graveyard. A tempest whooshed into Charlie's eye sockets, blurring his vision. He blinked. When his vision returned, he saw the bird's neck extend, awkwardly twist, then the creature's supernatural eyes locked with Charlie's.

Hisssss!

'I know what you are!' yelled Charlie.

Sweat dripped down Charlie's forehead. His red-raw fingers burned from the ice. He changed his grip.

'You're the demon!' he screamed.

Aaaaaaark. Aaaaaaark.

The bird screeched the loudest bloodcurdling squawk that Charlie had ever heard, like a piercing alarm, warning every living thing on earth that it was about to die. The raven's bulging eyes changed colour, from yellow, to red, back to yellow again. A blustering wind engulfed the tower. Charlie swung around the pole in a loop.

Then a flash of light burst from the core of the creature. Charlie watched the raven span its massive leathery wings. Charlie saw two wings, then three wings. He saw double. He saw triple. He blinked his eyelids again. The raven changed form. Emerging from the raven's body came a dark evil spirit, in the shape of a horrid skeleton with scraggy wings protruding from behind.

Through rotten fangs, the creature smiled unnervingly down at Charlie. It floated across the spire and came to a standing position on one of the three crowns. Scrawny black feathers fluttered like sheets around its skeletal bones. Lifting up its arm towards the stars and with warped long fingernails the creature clawed at Descartes' book.

'Give me the book!' shouted Charlie. He dangled from the pole.

The skeletal head of the monster twitched, its neck extended further and the beast's face loomed closer and closer to Charlie.

Hisssss!

Yellow eyes, with missing pupils, glared at Charlie.

Charlie tightened his grip on the pole. 'Why are you here? Why are you in Descartes' mind?'

'Because I can be!' roared the being.

'I know all about you,' said Charlie. 'You're feeding off the ideas in Descartes' book, trying to control his mind.'

'It's too late for Descartes. It was all over for him when he started questioning everything. He didn't know if he was thinking his thoughts, or if they were mine.' Rotten fangs beamed. 'The more Descartes doubted, the more powerful I became.'

'You have crushed him!' screamed Charlie.

'He served his purpose. Descartes' ideas were a good energy source to start with, but now I have found a better source — thanks to your grandfather.'

'Leave Ted out of this.'

'Your grandfather is a fool!'

'Ted's not a fool!' shouted Charlie.

'Yes, but he is.' The beast snarled through its spiked incisors. 'Your grandfather thinks you can stop me — just by retrieving this book. But you can't.' The creature tossed the book right at Charlie's head. 'I don't need this book anymore.'

With one hand clenching the pole, Charlie threw out his other arm and caught it in his palm. 'You're a monster,' shouted Charlie. 'You made Ted and his friends really sick!'

'Yes, I did.' The demon screeched out a tormenting laugh.

'Why?' yelled Charlie.

The demon quadrupled in size. 'When I realised I could jump from the mind to the soul and back again, the Eternal World became within my reach. It was there I found out about the Eternal Key. The best energy source of all. But I knew you had it. You lived in the physical world – out of my grasp. So, I devised a plan — get your grandfather to bring you, and the Key, to me.'

Horrified, Charlie stared at the creature.

'I visited your grandfather often, sucking him of his energy. He was a tough nut to start off with. He didn't call on you at first. Not until I started zapping his friends of their energy too.'

Charlie's fist clenched the pole tighter.

'And now, I have your little Key.'

Inflating its wiry wings even wider, the creature extended out a feathery limb exposing two claw-like fingernails holding the Key, silhouetted against the full moon. The beast grinned, flashing its fangs. The Key dangled in front of Charlie's nose.

'I can go anywhere now, take over anyone's mind, physical world or Eternal World. I am a time traveller.'

A lightning bolt blasted from the skeleton's fingertips. It struck the pole of the three crowns, zapping Charlie's hand.

Whoosh.

He lost his grip.

Charlie's body thumped down the steeple.

Bang. Bang. Bang.

His body hit every copper tile on the way down.

19

THE PRAYER

'Aarrgh!' Charlie screamed.

With one hand, he caught a support beam just above the viewing platform. Nine floors high, he dangled from the timber like a broken twig.

'Hold on!' shouted Belle from the platform underneath.

'Here.' Charlie tossed Descartes' book at Belle. 'Put it in your coat — I'm going back up.'

'No Charlie!' shrieked Belle.

'I have to get the Key!'

Splinters from the timber beam punctured Charlie's hands. His fingertips oozed blood and seeped under his nails. He glanced down at the courtyard and saw the guard with the musket. Other guards were now streaming into the square and they too fired at the birds.

Poomb. Poomb. Poomb.

With all his strength, Charlie swung his body up, back onto the roof of the spire. He started scaling the copper plates again.

'You *are* stupid, aren't you?' The skeletal demon laughed. 'You shouldn't have dropped that Key.'

'I didn't drop it,' roared Charlie. 'You stole it — now give it back!'

The demon snarled.

Charlie clambered up the plates, his gaze never left the bulging eyes of the creature. When he reached the metal rod, he grabbed it with both hands.

'Give me my Key!' he yelled. 'It's not going to work for you, I'm the Keyholder!'

Hissss!

'Yes, but it will, if I control your mind!' The vulture's laser sharp eyes delivered Charlie a piercing glare.

In that instant, a thunderbolt shot out from the creature and smacked across the eerie night. The demon outstretched its wings and bellowed a deafening screech that drilled a hole in Charlie's head. The pain was agonising, like someone had rammed a pole-vault through his brain.

'Your mind is coming to me!' The creature's

ALI GRAY

harrowing laughter roared past the castle's turrets, down the depths of the valley, until it had reached the darkest corners of the forest.

'Aarrgh!' Charlie pressed his ears hard.

'I will destroy you!' the creature snarled.

'You can't!' Charlie's head throbbed. His vision blurred. Dizziness took charge of his senses and his grip around the pole loosened.

That thing is taking over my mind, he thought. *It's actually winning.*

Laughter rattled the skies.

Charlie tried to fight it. *I can't let it. I can't let it.* His thoughts blurred. His mind started moving in and out of consciousness. With his fingers barely holding the pole, Charlie's legs crumpled underneath him.

'Charlie!' screamed Belle from the platform underneath. 'Hold the pole!'

'You can't save him!' snarled the creature.

One by one, Charlie felt his fingers lifting from the metal pole. And he knew he wasn't the one doing it.

'You are going to fall!' cried Belle. 'Hold the pole!'

Accepting his fate, Charlie's brain went in and out of a painful haze. *Ted help me. Please help.* Memories flashed through his mind. He saw Ted's ashen face and the dark rings circling his eyes. He saw the faces in the sky. He saw the man with the melon. He saw the little girl in the pink dress, sitting on the pew in the church. He heard the little girl recite her prayer. Maybe he should pray too? He started whispering the little girl's prayer in Latin, over and over and over. 'Cogito ergo sum… cogito ergo sum… cogito ergo sum…'

'Why are you speaking in Latin?' shouted Belle.

Charlie didn't know why he was speaking in Latin. He just kept on praying — over and over again.

'Cogito ergo sum… cogito ergo sum… cogito ergo sum…'

As he recited the prayer, the mist in his mind began to clear. He could feel the strength return to his fingers. He tightened his grip on the pole.

'Cogito ergo sum… cogito ergo sum…'

His voice became louder and louder. He felt stronger and stronger.

He yelled to Belle, 'What does it mean? What does *cogito ergo sum* mean?'

'Cogito ergo sum,' whispered Belle to herself. 'I think therefore I am.' She screamed back to Charlie. 'I think therefore I am!'

Charlie's eyes widened. The fog in his head evaporated in an instant.

'Of course!' he shouted. 'Of course! It's not a prayer. It's a thought. It is Descartes' thought. *I THINK — THEREFORE I AM!*'

A flash of terror stretched across the demon's emaciated face. The creature crunched over and held its gut as though it had been poisoned by something deadly.

With renewed strength, Charlie gripped the metal pole tightly. He shifted his hands up the pole and lifted his crumpled legs from the copper plates. Standing on the tip of the spire, he stared daggers at the demon. Like Charlie's glare was causing pain, the creature rose from the crowns. It tried to flap its ailing wings, but it couldn't fly. It just hovered awkwardly above Charlie's head.

'You cannot take over my mind!' Charlie waved his fist at the demon. 'Because I am the one doing the thinking!'

'And if I think…' belted Charlie. 'I am — I exist, and you don't!'

A deafening scream roared from the demon's fang-filled mouth. Thunder raged throughout the skies and a lightning bolt came from a star and struck the Key in the demon's claws. The force propelled the gold object high into the sky. Before Charlie's eyes, the demon started to crumble like a charred stick of wood. It shrivelled smaller and smaller, until it was the size of a tennis ball.

Boom.

The ball exploded into a firework and disappeared amongst the stars.

Charlie flew from the spire and dived for the Key, catching it in mid-air. His body bounced down the copper plates. Rolling, buckling and plunging. He shut his eyes and held his breath. His body tumbled like a weed down the spire.

A tiny pair of hands stretched out from a timber beam, underneath the spire. To Charlie's relief, Belle hauled him in.

Thud!

Charlie landed on the viewing platform.

In that second, an electrical current surged from the Key. It shot up Charlie's arm and infiltrated his body. The force of the current told Charlie something strange was about to happen. He grabbed Belle's hand. A white light flashed in front of his eyes.

Gripping the Key tightly, Charlie pressed it against his heart. He saw a white glossy locker, with green slime on the door. The green ooze on the cabinet started to retrace up the door, towards the lightbulb on top. It poured back into the globe and the broken glass fused together, as if the bulb had never smashed.

Then Charlie's body became sucked up by a ventricle. As he twisted through the tube, he felt Belle's tiny hand in his palm. He squeezed it. A wall of pumping veins and a network of red arteries appeared in front of his eyes. He heard the rhythmic beating of blood. He sensed a slimy grey film stretching across his body. The whiff of raw flesh made its way down into his lungs. He could see Belle.

He tried to speak to her — but he couldn't. Words didn't come.

Suddenly, he heard a gushing sound. Animal spirits had taken hold. Charlie heard an onslaught of familiar roars — tigers, lions, bears. A violent gust pulled him down a tube. It spat him onto floorboards. He landed with a thump.

20

THE APARTMENT

Charlie slowly lifted his head. His neck creaked. Belle lay next to him. Stumbling to his feet, his whole body ached. He reached for Belle's hand and pulled her into a standing position in the middle of Descartes' apartment.

The moonlight filtered through the ice resting against the windowpane outside. The rays illuminated Descartes' face, who was sleeping peacefully in his chair. Belle dashed over to the Frenchman. She sat on the arm of the chair and watched Descartes in his slumber.

'The book,' said Charlie. 'Have you still got the book?'

Belle reached under her coat and pulled the book

from a pocket. She gave it to Charlie.

He stepped forward and carefully placed it into Descartes' warm hands.

'Your book, Descartes,' whispered Charlie. 'We got it back.'

The Frenchman stirred. His eyelids fluttered open and his dark eyes twinkled. He rubbed his thumb across the spine of the book and lifted it to eye level. He opened the front cover.

'Thank you,' said Descartes. 'Thank you for all you have done for me, Monsieur Charlie.'

'Belle helped me,' said Charlie. 'She's amazing.'

A smile crossed Descartes' face. He nodded at Belle and her green irises sparkled back.

'*Meditations*.' Descartes read the hand-written title. His long slender fingers flicked across the pages.

'Monsieur Charlie, Mademoiselle Belle, you have returned my most important work.'

Tears surged in the Frenchman's brown eyes. Droplets ran down his cheekbones and stopped on the corners of his quivering lips. Gently, he closed the book and rested it on his chest.

'Thank you,' he said again. 'I can retreat to my house as my foundations are now stable — and someday, I know, I will re-unite with my dearest Francine…'

With that, the Frenchman shut his eyelids. Still clutching the book to his heart, he leaned back in his armchair.

'I can see her now, you know... in her little pink dress.'

Charlie's mind flashed back to the church, the girl in the pink dress. *It was Francine*, he thought, *in the centre of Descartes mind, helping us fight the demon.*

'My work is done,' said Descartes finally.

Charlie watched the Frenchman's chest rise and fall. Soon his breathing became heavier and shallow snores reverberated across the room.

Heat coming from the Key tingled Charlie's hand. He knew it was time to leave. He glanced at Belle and sadness rumbled inside.

'I have to go,' he said.

'Why?' said Belle. 'Why do you not stay with us here for a while?'

'No,' said Charlie, 'I have a family at home — they need me.'

This, Charlie knew Belle would understand.

Belle's green eyes went glassy.

'You are brave,' she said.

'So are you,' said Charlie. 'Look after yourself — and your family.'

'I will,' she sniffed. 'I will do my best.'

Charlie stood quietly for a short moment and watched Belle cry. Then he did something he wouldn't normally do. He went to Belle. He put his arms around her coat and felt her little body shaking underneath. He hugged her tightly.

'Goodbye, Belle,' Charlie whispered.

The softness of Belle's skin pressed against his face. All of a sudden, Charlie's heart became heavier. *I really like Belle.* He thought. *I am going to miss her.*

'Goodbye, Charlie,' said Belle.

Charlie stepped back, closed his eyes and squeezed the Key in his hand. He started to wish. He wished for his country. He wished for his time. He wished for the bathroom of the school hall. The Key began to glow. He watched Belle, Descartes and the room disappear.

All he could see now was white light — pure light. A vacuum of wind engulfed Charlie. He tightened his grip on the Key and felt his body lifting.

Whoosh.

Charlie launched into space. A gale ripped through his hair. He flew like a bird. He flew like a raven. His arms glided without effort. He soared higher and higher, to altitudes not possible to reach. Higher and higher, to places that didn't exist. On top of the world, he saw everything.

The cuts on his fingertips, the punctures in his hands, the gash in his ankle, all vanished. A pool of calm came over him, smothering him, like a warm gentle cloud. But then the wind changed temperature. His body changed direction. No support anywhere. He plummeted into a free-fall.

21

THE GRAPH

Opening his eyes, Charlie saw a wash basin rise above his head. He watched the walls of the bathroom fold upwards, and the roof snap down on top of the walls, turning the bathroom back into a box. He lifted his head from the hard tiles of the floor and rubbed it.

'Charlie!' yelled Mrs. Grimshaw. 'What is going on in there?'

'Errr… sorry Mrs. Grimshaw,' yelled back Charlie. 'I'm coming.'

Slowly, Charlie unravelled his fingers and examined the Key. Under the etching of the sun, he studied the lines of the cross. Not luminous anymore, just back to a normal shiny gold.

Grinning, he clambered to his feet, straightened his tie, and popped the Key into his blazer pocket. He opened the bathroom door. 'Hi there.'

Mrs. Grimshaw narrowed her eyes. 'I was starting to worry about you.'

'I'm fine,' whispered Charlie.

The teacher waved Charlie towards the direction of his seat.

As Charlie sat into position, he noticed the clock at the front of the hall — five minutes past eleven o'clock. He suddenly remembered something Ted had told him when he went to Ancient Greece. 'In the Eternal World time doesn't exist'.

The Eternal Key belongs to the Eternal World, he thought, *so when I travel with the Key time doesn't change – because it doesn't exist.*

He flicked the pages of the exam paper to Question Eight.

With one hour to go Charlie re-read the question. He knew what to do. He counted the points along the X axis until he got to twenty-two, then he counted sixteen lines above. He marked the spot with his pencil and drew a line from this point to the last point, confident he had got the answer right. He finished the rest of the paper in no time.

'Pencils down,' said Mrs. Grimshaw.

Charlie came out of the exam room and stretched out his back as the sun's rays bombarded his face. He grinned at the royal blue sky with not a cloud in sight.

I'm in my time, he thought. He started walking towards home.

As Charlie meandered along a gravel footpath, he noticed the spire of the church on the hill. He decided to take the long route home and bounced up the steps towards the church. Tiny stones shot from underneath his sneakers as he climbed the rise. He opened the gate and strolled into the church's grassy yard.

'Good afternoon, son.' A gardener trimmed a hedge with shears. 'Lovely day for it.'

'Hello,' grinned Charlie. 'It sure is.'

Bypassing the church, Charlie took the side path and entered the cemetery at the rear. He strolled to the far corner of the graveyard, that bordered a horse paddock.

At Ted's glistening headstone, Charlie dropped to his knees. Specks in the granite glittered like diamonds and reflected onto Charlie's face. He read the inscription, *'Ted Bailey, aged seventy two. My soul is free at last.'*

Fumbling in his blazer, Charlie pulled out a piece of note paper and a pencil. He flattened the paper on the edge of the grave and smoothed out the crinkles with his palm. With the pencil, he drew a line horizontally across the page and marked it with an X. He then drew a vertical line that crossed the other line and marked it *Y*.

Under the horizonal line, Charlie started writing numbers across, *-5, -4, -3* and so on until he reached *0* where the vertical line crossed. Then he wrote *1, 2, 3* along the horizontal line until he reached *5*. He did the same along the vertical line starting at the bottom, *-5, -4, -3…* until he reached *0*, and then he kept on going until he got to *5*.

As he wrote the numbers, he whispered, 'Ted, I don't know if you know this, but when I was in Sweden, I found out that Descartes invented the graph.'

He heaved a sigh, tears formed in his eyes. 'So, I thought I would come here and show you how much I miss you.'

Charlie started to put crosses on the paper. 'You see Ted, when you were alive, I didn't miss you at all because you were with me most of the time.' So, I was at point *zero*. That by the way was the location of Francine's grave, Descartes' daughter.'

With pencil in hand, Charlie put a cross at point *zero*. 'Then when you got sick and couldn't meet me anymore at the museum. I missed you this much.' He put a cross at the coordinates *three* points along the X axis and *three* points up the Y axis.

'Then you got really sick and went into hospital and you couldn't talk at all. I missed you this much.' Charlie put a cross at the coordinates *five* points along the X axis and *five* points up the Y axis.

'But when you died — that's when I missed you the most.' Charlie heaved.

Charlie drew a line with the pencil that passed through all the crosses he had drawn so far, but then he continued the line until the lead had run off the page. He tossed the pencil to the ground. Hunching over the piece of paper, he started crying. His chest swelled and he could barely breathe.

'So here, Ted.' Charlie wiped his eyes. He tried to gather his thoughts. 'This graph is for you.'

Still shaking, he folded the piece of paper carefully and placed it behind some lavender flowers propped up in a vase, resting against the headstone. He rose to his feet, wiped his tears with his blazer sleeve and turned away from Ted's grave. He began to head for home.

A sudden gust of wind whipped up the dirt at his feet. The flurry was so strong, Charlie twisted his neck to view Ted's resting place one more time, hoping the vase hadn't toppled over. But when he turned, he saw the piece of paper fly away with the gale.

'Hey!' he shouted. 'That's for Ted!'

The wind thrashed the paper higher.

'Hey, that's Ted's,' he shouted again. 'Bring it back!'

Dodging the headstones, Charlie chased the paper

across the cemetery, leaping high into the air, trying to snatch it.

'Damn wind!' He couldn't quite reach it.

The paper glided over the churchyard, caught like a leaf, in some kind of unnatural airstream. But it was no use.

Charlie stopped running and watched the paper rocket skyward and disappear behind the church.

But then something weird happened. A burst of sunlight flashed from the sun and exploded onto the church's steeple. White light. Pure light.

The spire started to change colour. It went from a dull blue-grey to a brilliant sparkling gold and glistened like a star. Almost magical. Dumbstruck, Charlie stood in wonder. He grinned at the image.

'Like gold itself,' he whispered.

Then, even stranger things happened. Images of people appeared on the spire. A girl in a heavy brown coat blew Charlie a kiss — it was Belle.

A man nodded politely towards Charlie and held up a book — Descartes. A little girl in a pink dress ran to Descartes and jumped up into his arms — the girl from the church, Francine.

Next moment, Ted came into the image. Larger than life and a picture of health, Ted flashed a smile wider than a lake. With his arm high over his head, he threw Charlie a huge wave, clearly proud of his grandson.

Then, behind Ted, appeared a thousand happy faces all glowing on the spire.

Charlie punched the air with his fist. His face beamed like the sun.

'Hey, Ted!' he shouted. 'That's the real colour of the spire!'

ABOUT THE AUTHOR

Ali Gray lives in Sydney, Australia with her husband and their two daughters. Descartes' Demon is Ali's second novel in the *Eternal Key* series. To find out more about Ali, visit www.aligray.com.au.

Made in the USA
Middletown, DE
19 January 2022

59135357R00094